Chula Vista Institute of Religion
845 Otay Lakes Rd.
Chula Vista, CA 91910

WE'LL BRING THE WORLD HIS TRUTH

We'll Bring the World His Truth

His Truth

Missionary Adventures from Around the World

DEAN HUGHES

AND

TOM HUGHES

DESERET BOOK COMPANY
SALT LAKE CITY, UTAH

Library of Congress Cataloging-in-Publication Data

Hughes, Dean, 1943–
   We'll bring the world his truth : missionary adventures from around the world / Dean Hughes and Tom Hughes.
       p.   cm.
   Summary: Presents the lives and accomplishments of Latter-day Saint missionaries past and present.
   ISBN 1-57345-090-1 (hardback)
   1. Missionaries—Biography—Juvenile literature. 2. Church of Jesus Christ of Latter-day Saints—Missions—Juvenile literature. 3. Mormon church—Missions—Juvenile literature. 4. Mormons —Biography—Juvenile literature. [1. Missionaries. 2. Mormons. 3. Church of Jesus Christ of Latter-day Saints—Missions.]
I. Hughes, Tom, 1968–   . II. Title.
BX8661.H74   1995   95-30975
                                             CIP
                                             AC

Printed in the United States of America
10 9   8   7   6   5   4   3   2   1

CONTENTS

CONTENTS

PREFACE

On a November day in 1989, I was sitting at my computer, writing, when the phone rang. I recognized the voice of my son, Tom, as he said, "Dad, have you heard?"

"Heard what?" I asked. But my son couldn't speak. He had begun to cry. "Heard what?" I asked again.

"They're taking the Wall down," he finally managed to say. And then he really broke down. And I began to cry too.

The wall he was talking about, of course, was the Berlin Wall. My son had recently returned from a mission to Hamburg, Germany, and his first assignment had been in Berlin. He had learned how much the German people hated that wall—that terrible division of their country. Later, as an assistant to the mission president, Tom had driven to Berlin many times, always passing through the East German "corridor" to get there. But by that time, Germany was *his* country. And he too hated that wall, that division.

Tom came home from his mission just a few months before the Wall was torn down. I had arrived for my mission in Germany about a year after the Wall had been built. I experienced the pain that Germans felt about the division when that pain was new. Germany became, and has remained, my country too.

So Tom and I cried for joy together that day. And one more time, our shared missionary experience had brought us close.

In 1987, when Tom had called home from college to tell his mother and me that he had his mission call, I was stunned when he told us where he was going. Tom, I think, was expecting instant excitement. Instead he heard a long silence, and then, "Well, you'll love the bread." But if I hesitated, it was only because I knew what he was in for. Germany is not an easy place to serve.

I had begun my mission in September 1962. Tom left the Missionary Training

Center and flew to Germany in September 1987, twenty-five years later. As he struggled with the language and the adjustment to missionary life, I remembered my first October, my first Thanksgiving, my first Christmas. I knew exactly what he was going through.

Tom survived a hard first winter—just as I had done. The winter of 1962–63 was one of the coldest in European history. Honest. Tom thinks I exaggerate, but I tell him to check the records. I will admit, however, that he spent his first winter far up north, where the wind blows cold off the North Sea. What was worse, though, was that he worked in a little town that hadn't had a convert baptism in years. By the time Tom had served eight months, he hadn't even *seen* a baptism, let alone performed one.

Tom wrote letters that were fairly upbeat, but between the lines were his frustrations. I felt the emotion in those white spaces. I was reliving my mission, and every night I was praying that what had happened to me would eventually happen to him.

Then things started to change. He was called to be a senior companion, and spring came—but more than anything, he began to mature. He found three young adults, all friends, who accepted the gospel and were baptized. That got him *begeistert* (a German word that means "spirited"). His testimony was deepening, and so was his commitment. He was thinking less of himself and more of the people he was trying to find and teach.

Then one day something remarkable happened. Tom was writing letters on his "preparation day." Around the room were some very old issues of *Der Stern* magazine—a German LDS publication. As he was writing, he happened to notice that the magazine he had set his writing paper on was a particularly old one. He flipped open the back page and noticed a picture of President Ezra Taft Benson with the mission president and other leaders of the South German Mission. That rang a bell, and Tom studied the picture more closely. Then he realized—he was looking at a picture of me. I was one of the missionaries. That day he wrote home:

> I don't think I've ever felt closer to my own dad than I do looking at this picture. . . . Somehow it really has struck home that this is an experience that we have

totally in common, and it is something we can relate to on completely common ground without the father/son gap that can sometimes creep into the tightest relationship. For the first time I have realized completely that your suggestions don't come from being my dad, but rather from an experienced missionary who also went through the German refiner's fire. Somehow, it gives me the feeling that I'm carrying on a great work that the first Elder Hughes began in Germany before any ideas about the second Elder Hughes had ever been conceived. And then I think what a truly majestic work my Father in Heaven started so many forevers ago, and I just become overwhelmed with the feeling of a "family tie" to my Heavenly Dad.

Needless to say, that's another time I cried. Tom served a fine mission. He and I cherish our shared experience. But we know we are only two little specks in a great movement. We have joined forces with Peter, Paul, Joseph Smith, Parley P. Pratt, Matthew Cowley—and all the thousands of modern-day missionaries. Each mission is a powerful experience—challenging, inspiring, discouraging, exciting, and all the rest. But all those missions, joined together, create a massive effort to change the hearts and minds of people, to bring them to Christ.

This book is, first of all, a glimpse at the amazing variety of missionary experiences. But Tom and I hope you will also notice the patterns that link these episodes. Every missionary has to grow into his or her mission. And perhaps no one has ever gotten through the whole experience without self-doubt and discouragement. Still, what is also common to almost every mission is the growth that comes in meeting those challenges. Along with the stories of conversion, healings, and miracles—experienced by those who are taught—notice what happens in these stories to those who teach.

When Peter accepted his call, Christ told him and his brother Andrew, "Come ye after me, and I will make you *to become* fishers of men." (Mark 1:17; emphasis added.) Peter was not transformed immediately. He accepted the call, but he had to *become* a missionary. And he struggled with that. For a long time he didn't seem to grasp the fullness of what Christ meant to the world. He battled with doubt, and at times he lost faith. And even after all he experienced, he turned his back on his Lord and denied Him three times. Still, through all these tests, Peter was growing and *becoming*. And after Christ was gone, Peter finally began to act with power. When a beggar asked alms of him, he told the man,

"Silver and gold have I none; but such as I have give I thee: In the name of Jesus Christ of Nazareth rise up and walk." (Acts 3:6.) Then he reached down and pulled the man up, and the man did walk.

Peter had become like Christ. He was doing what he had seen Christ do. He had the power to heal the sick. His faith was full and deep. He had *become* a fisher of men.

And so the tradition has continued. While I was serving in the city of Ulm, a woman came to me and asked to be healed of tuberculosis. I was twenty years old. I wasn't Peter. I wasn't Joseph Smith or Parley P. Pratt or Matthew Cowley. How could *I* say, "Rise up and walk"? But three other elders and I fasted, and then we went to Sister Feile's house and administered to her. And she was healed.

She was healed of tuberculosis, and the truth is, I was amazed. But I was *becoming* a fisher of men, and so were the other elders who had watched Sister Feile's faith create a miracle for us to witness.

Tom had similar experiences. And through those experiences we are joined. We are part of the most important, far-reaching, exciting work in the history of the world. This book is only a series of snapshots extracted from a grand moving picture. But these stories are samples of all the marvelous experiences that many thousands have shared as they have *become* fishers of men.

In his 1975 book *The Expanding Church*, Spencer Palmer predicted that in forty years 50,000 missionaries would be serving. But the Church reached that figure in only twenty years. In other words, the work is not just continuing but picking up power and speed.

No one should go on a mission without understanding that he or she will face hardships, tests, adjustments, and soul-searching discouragement. But if young people—or couples—begin their missions, like Peter, not yet as full of faith and strength as they want to be, yet ready to meed the demands, they will experience the greatest growth and satisfaction of their lives. They may be happy to return home at the end, just as Tom and I were, but they will know they are changed inside—and that their labors have contributed to the greatest work ever under-taken.

DEAN HUGHES

1

Parley P. Pratt in Canada

Missionaries in The Church of Jesus Christ of Latter-day Saints have always set out with the same goal: to find and teach those people who are willing to accept the restored gospel of Jesus Christ. The nature of the work has changed little, but conditions and methods, of course, have changed a great deal. Modern missionaries submit their papers and then wait excitedly for an official call, by letter, from the prophet. In 1836, Parley P. Pratt received his call in a very different way.

Elder Pratt, who was an apostle in the Church had been thinking it was time for him to serve another mission, but he was in debt from having served so often in the past. He needed to build a decent home and get his ailing wife, Thankful, settled in better circumstances. But one of his fellow apostles, Elder Heber C. Kimball, dropped by his house and prophesied that if Elder Pratt would serve a mission at this time, his wife would be healed of her illnesses and would bear a son whose name would also be Parley. "Arise, therefore," Elder Kimball proclaimed, "and go forth in the ministry, nothing doubting. Take no thoughts for your debts, nor the necessaries of life, for the Lord will supply you with abundant means for all things."

Then Elder Kimball made his prophecy more specific. Elder Pratt was to go to Toronto, Canada, and there he would "find a people prepared for the fullness of the gospel." Further, Elder Kimball promised, "Thou shalt organize the Church among them, and it shall spread thence into the regions round about."

For Parley and Thankful Pratt, this was a wonderful promise. For ten years Thankful had been sick, and she had not been able to have children. They had also had many financial problems. But few people have ever possessed the faith of this couple. There was no question in their minds whether Elder Pratt should go.

1

The first sign that the blessing from Elder Kimball would come true occurred when a Brother Nickerson offered to cover part of Elder Pratt's travel expenses to Toronto. The two traveled together by stagecoach to Niagara Falls, and then they walked for two days to the city of Hamilton. Elder Pratt stayed for a short time in Hamilton and preached, but he was determined to get to Toronto.

The walk around Lake Ontario was long and difficult, but steamboat passage cost two dollars, and Elder Pratt didn't have any money. Elder Pratt went into the woods and prayed for help. When he returned to Hamilton, a stranger approached him and asked who he was and where he was going. Elder Pratt explained his mission, and the man immediately offered him ten dollars. He also gave Elder Pratt a letter of introduction to a gentleman there named John Taylor. Elder Pratt was grateful for the money, but the letter turned out to be of even greater importance.

When Elder Pratt arrived in Toronto, he went directly to the Taylor house. John Taylor was not overly excited about the visit, but he did invite Elder Pratt in. Elder Pratt spent the next day searching for a place to preach—with no success. Upon returning to the Taylor home, however, he overheard a conversation between Mrs. Taylor and a visitor named Mrs. Walton. When Mrs. Taylor said that Elder Pratt was with them, and that he claimed to be sent by the Lord, Mrs. Walton said, "I now understand the feelings and spirit which brought me to your house at this time."

Mrs. Walton went on to explain that she had been washing clothes when she felt inspired to go for a walk, even though she was tired. She decided to visit her sister, but on the way there she passed the Taylor home and felt prompted to stop and go in. She told herself she would see the Taylors on the way back, but the Spirit told her to do it then. Now she felt certain that Elder Pratt was the reason.

Mrs. Walton extended an invitation for Elder Pratt to come and stay with her family and to use two large rooms in her house as a place to hold meetings. She then set out to gather a group to her home that very night.

Elder Pratt soon learned that Mrs. Walton and her friends had been prepared for the gospel. When he told them about Joseph Smith and the Restoration, the Spirit bore witness to them that the message was true. When the meeting ended, everyone in the room asked for baptism. Elder Pratt told them to wait just a little and learn more, and in the meantime he continued to preach to others who were friends of the Taylors and the Waltons.

Elder Parley P. Pratt

At one meeting the group raised questions about whether the true principles had been lost from the earth, never to return. Others suggested that they pray that the heavens be opened by new revelation. For three nights, Elder Pratt preached to this group and explained that the heavens had already been opened, just as the people in the group hoped they would be.

Mrs. Walton joined the Church with many of her friends, and so did John Taylor and his family. Brother Taylor soon became Elder Pratt's assistant. Many more people in the area entered the Church, all of whom seemed well prepared for the message brought to them. And the reason for the urgency of Elder Pratt's mission became clear in time. John Taylor became a great leader and would eventually serve as the third President of the Church. But even before his baptism, he helped Parley fulfill Elder Kimball's prophecy. He introduced him to another family that became important in Church history. Mary Fielding, who joined the Church with her brother Joseph and her sister Mercy, later married Hyrum Smith, the Prophet's brother. Hyrum and Mary's son, Joseph F. Smith, would serve as the sixth President of the Church, and his son, Joseph Fielding Smith, would become the tenth President.

Elder Pratt did not live long enough to see John Taylor become President of the Church, but he saw the Lord's promises to him come true. He had found the people Elder Kimball had prophesied he would find, and they had accepted the gospel. His financial needs had also been met. And back in Kirtland, Ohio, Thankful gave birth to a baby boy. She named him Parley.

For further reading, see Parley P. Pratt, *Autobiography of Parley P. Pratt* (Salt Lake City: Deseret Book Co., 1975); and B. H. Roberts, *The Life of John Taylor* (Salt Lake City: Bookcraft, 1963).

2

WILFORD WOODRUFF'S DREAM

Wilford Woodruff joined the Church in 1833. He quickly became an important leader and was called to be an apostle in 1838. From the beginning he had a great wish to preach the gospel. His first mission, in 1835, was to Arkansas and Tennessee, where he traveled with Elder Henry Brown. The mission began in danger because the elders chose to walk through the state of Missouri, where not long before the Saints had been driven out. Governor Lilburn W. Boggs had issued an order that all Mormons leave the state or be *exterminated*, and many Missourians were still ready to carry out that order.

What Elder Woodruff learned, however, was that the Lord was not going to allow this mission to fail. He would protect the elders from their enemies— sometimes in amazing ways.

In Arkansas, the missionaries looked for a family named Akeman. The Akemans were members of the Church who had been driven out of Jackson County, Missouri, but had gone south rather than east to Illinois, as most of the Saints had done. Elders Woodruff and Brown camped one night in the woods, about two miles from where they had learned the Akemans were living. They planned to visit the family the next day. But during the night, Wilford Woodruff had a very strange dream.

In the dream, an angel commanded the missionaries to follow a straight path. The path led to the door of a house. The path had a wall on either side, so that the only way to follow the path was through the door. Elder Woodruff recorded the details of the dream in his diary:

> I opened the door and saw the room was filled with large serpents, and I shuddered at the sight. My companion said he would not go into the room for fear of the serpents. I told him I would try to go through the room though they killed me, for the Lord commanded it. As I stepped into the room the serpents coiled themselves

5

up, and raised their heads some two feet from the floor, to spring at me. There was one much larger than the rest, in the center of the room, which raised his head nearly as high as mine and made a spring at me. At that instant I felt as though nothing but the power of God could save me, and I stood still. Just before the serpent reached me he dropped dead at my feet; all the rest dropped dead, swelled up, turned black, [burst] open, took fire and were consumed before my eyes, and we went through the room unharmed, thanking God for our deliverance.

When Elder Woodruff awoke, he was certain that this intense dream would soon prove to be significant. He warned his companion that something strange was about to happen to them.

When the two elders reached the Akeman home that day, they learned that Brother Akeman had turned against the Church. He was full of bitterness and hatred. He promised to raise a mob to drive the missionaries out of the area. But an older couple named Hubbel, who lived in the neighborhood, had read the Book of Mormon and believed. The two missionaries decided, in spite of the danger, to stay and teach them. They even helped Mr. Hubbel clear land for planting.

After about three weeks, Elder Woodruff decided it was time to visit Mr. Akeman and to bear testimony to him. But on the way, he felt a "deep, gloomy frame of mind" come over him. And then, when he arrived at the house, he saw Mr. Akeman through the open door. He was walking back and forth nervously. Elder Woodruff asked whether he was well, but Mr. Akeman said he had never felt better.

Elder Woodruff took this chance to testify that the Book of Mormon was true and that it was wrong for Mr. Akeman to oppose the work of God. But Mr. Akeman became angry. He insulted Elder Woodruff and other Church leaders, and he denounced the Church as being false.

Elder Woodruff felt nothing but evil in the house, so he turned to leave. Mr. Akeman followed close behind, and Elder Woodruff wondered whether he was in danger from this angry man. After walking a short distance, however, Elder Woodruff felt a sudden sense of well-being—a sense that he was safe. As he continued walking, and as Mr. Akeman reached the same point where Elder Woodruff had suddenly felt safe, Mr. Akeman dropped to the ground. Elder Woodruff heard this but didn't look back. He hurried on.

Back at the Hubbels' home, Elder Woodruff sat down to dinner. He had only just begun to eat when a man on a horse rode up to the house. He cried out: "Mr. Akeman is dead. I want you to go there immediately."

Elder Woodruff left his dinner and hurried back to the Akeman home. When he looked at Mr. Akeman's body, he saw that it was so swollen that the skin seemed ready to break open. And then he understood. His dream had been fulfilled. Mr. Akeman was the great serpent. Elder Woodruff had tried to warn him to repent, but instead he had come after the apostle. At that moment he had fallen to the ground, dead.

Elder Woodruff could have felt resentment toward Mr. Akeman, but instead he preached the funeral sermon for his former brother. He and his companion stayed on two more weeks, and they baptized the Hubbels. During that

Elder Wilford Woodruff

time, Elder Woodruff reported that several more of the anti-Mormon mob died suddenly. But that did not surprise him. He had seen his dream as a prophecy, and it was clear to him that it would be fulfilled. The Lord's work had to continue, and Elder Woodruff had a great destiny to fulfill. He would someday become the prophet of the Church.

For further reading, see Francis M. Gibbons, *Wilford Woodruff: Wondrous Worker, Prophet of God* (Salt Lake City: Deseret Book Co., 1988); Matthias F. Cowley, *Wilford Woodruff: History of His Life and Labors* (Salt Lake City: Bookcraft, 1964); and Thomas G. Alexander, *Things in Heaven and Earth: The Life and Times of Wilford Woodruff, a Mormon Prophet* (Salt Lake City: Signature Books, 1991).

3

GEORGE A. SMITH'S LOVE STORY

When we think of modern apostles, we picture mature men with great leadership experience. But that description does not fit the first apostles called by Joseph Smith. In fact, one of them, George A. Smith, a cousin to the Prophet, was only twenty-one when he was called. He was single, and when he wasn't serving missions, he still lived with his parents.

Elder Smith was also, in his own opinion, not exactly the "coolest" guy around. He was a very big man, and he had a way of stepping in the wrong places. Once, in 1840, while serving a mission in England with other apostles, he was staying with a member family. Trying to find his way to bed in the dark, he stepped on the family's poor cat and killed it. He felt horrible. That night he wrote in his diary—as he would also do on other occasions—how foolish he felt about his constant clumsiness.

George A. Smith's descriptions of himself are sometimes rather comical. He was seasick most of the way across the ocean, and he missed the fresh vegetables from his garden at home in Nauvoo. Upon arriving in England, he bought himself a tall, black hat in an attempt to look dignified, but his experience with Heber C. Kimball shows that *dignity* may not have been all that natural to him. He walked out with Elder Kimball through the Liverpool market, which he described as being "filled with fruits and vegetables of great variety and beauty from all climates. I never saw anything to equal it. . . . Brother Kimball said he would buy me anything I desired. I chose a large onion, which cost one penny. I ate it with a craving appetite and shed many tears over it."

Elder Smith was an apostle, but he was about the same age as most modern full-time missionaries. And he had some of the same feelings. Among those were homesickness and a lack of confidence in his own ability. Shortly after arriving in England, he wrote his parents: "I wish to be remembered to all the Saints and ask their prayers and faith, for I never needed them more. . . . I want to hear from you as I have received but one letter since I left home. I could tell you much if I could see you but I am not mighty in writing."

Later we hear his homesickness, between the lines, as he wrote: "I have received only one letter from you since I landed in England. . . . I have written several to you. . . . Write me a long letter. Tell me the general news, for you cannot imagine how much I want to hear from you."

The next passage in the same letter reveals some of his other hidden feelings. Elder Smith had more on his mind than merely his parents: "Tell Sister Bathsheba Bigler I have not exactly forgotten her, notwithstanding my bad memory; if she is married wish her much joy for me, and if she is single wish her much joy with me."

Yes, George A. Smith, the young apostle, had a girlfriend back home. And he was hoping, as so many missionaries have done since that time, that she would wait for him. He had met Bathsheba Bigler while he was on a previous mission, his third, in Shinnston, Virginia (now West Virginia). She was only sixteen at the time, but the two talked, and they promised each other that in three years they would marry. Three years had passed, but Elder Smith was very far from home. The Biglers now lived in Nauvoo, Illinois, as did George A.'s parents, but Elder Smith had found little time to write, and now he wondered whether some dandy in Nauvoo—someone less clumsy and more dignified—had stolen Bathsheba's heart.

Eventually, Elder Smith took a more direct approach and wrote to Bathsheba. His letter, however formal, shows how deep his commitment had remained:

> I take the liberty to inform you . . . that you are not forgotten. I keep you still in memory and the pleasant hours I have spent in your society are still remembered. . . . I have not written to you as I ought to have done. Will you please forgive me? . . . Truly if you and I come together, it will be because we were each other's in eternity. I remain your most faithful friend in a distant land. Write to me as soon as you get this.

Like most missionaries, past and present, Elder Smith didn't let his homesickness or his thoughts of the girl back home slow his work. On June 26, 1840, he wrote:

> I am on this day 23 years old, five thousand miles from home, [the] weather cold

9

and wet. . . . For the last twenty days I have been so busy with preaching, counseling, baptizing, confirming and teaching the people, that I have not had time to journalize any, and have seldom gone to bed before two o'clock in the morning as people were constantly in my room inquiring about the work of the Lord.

Elder Smith was growing and maturing. He was experiencing miracles and seeing *thousands* of new converts come into the Church. He was serving with men older than himself, but he was proving himself worthy of his great calling.

Elder George A. Smith

Still, however, he continued to worry about his weaknesses and failings.

A year after their arrival in England, most of the apostles met in Manchester to prepare for their return trip. They landed in New York on May 20, 1841, after being at sea for a month. It took Elder Smith six weeks to "preach his way home." There he was reunited with his family in Zarahemla, a little Mormon settlement across the river from Nauvoo. Two days later he crossed the Mississippi to visit Bathsheba and find out whether she still had any feelings for him. No doubt he approached her house with a pounding heart.

But she had waited. She was still committed to marry him.

Four years had passed since Sister Bigler and Elder Smith had met, so they didn't wait much longer. On Sunday, July 25, 1841, they were married. George A. Smith, whatever qualities he felt he lacked, had touched the heart of the pretty young Sister Bigler. Perhaps she had seen the goodness in this big man who saw so little to admire in himself. Or maybe she sensed his future greatness. Elder Smith would eventually serve in the First Presidency of the Church and become a fine leader, a good speaker, a truly great man.

The beauty of the Smiths' story is not only in their good marriage but also in the children and grandchildren that would come from their union. Bathsheba Smith would give birth to a son they would name John Henry Smith. He would also become an important leader in the Church. His son, George Albert Smith, would someday serve as President of the Church.

So theirs was a good love story. The best kind. One that lasts forever.

For further reading, see Merlo J. Pusey, *Builders of the Kingdom: George A. Smith, John Henry Smith, George Albert Smith* (Provo, Utah: Brigham Young University Press, 1981); and Zora Smith Jarvis, *Ancestry, Biography, and Family of George A. Smith* (Provo, Utah: Brigham Young University Press, 1962).

4

Orson Hyde—Dedicating the Holy Land

In the spring conference of 1840, in Nauvoo, Illinois, Elder Orson Hyde of the Quorum of the Twelve was called to travel to Jerusalem, there to dedicate the Holy Land for the gathering of the Jews. Joseph Smith had been instructed by the Lord that Jews from all over the world would create a homeland in Jerusalem and fulfill the prophecies in the scriptures.

Orson Hyde had been very sick, but he prepared himself for his mission. He already knew that it was his destiny to begin this important work. He had seen a vision, a month before, in which he traveled to London, Amsterdam, Constantinople, and then Jerusalem. He saw himself meeting with Jewish leaders and rabbis, learning about their religion and announcing that the time had come for the gathering to begin.

Elder Hyde was assigned a companion, John E. Page. The two made their ways separately to New York from Nauvoo and preached along the way. When Elder Hyde arrived in New York, nine months had passed since his mission call, and yet he arrived ahead of Elder Page. Elder Hyde received word from Joseph Smith that he was not pleased at the slow progress the missionaries were making. Elder Hyde was also anxious to set sail for Europe. He waited another month, but when Elder Page didn't arrive, he decided to get on with his long trip.

Elder Hyde followed the path he had seen in his vision. He landed in England and spent time with some of the other apostles who were completing their great mission in England. Elder Hyde sought out an important Jewish rabbi, Dr. Solomon Hirschell, but was unable to meet with him. And so he wrote Dr. Hirschell a long letter, describing the vision he had seen and encouraging the idea that the time for the gathering of Jews to Jerusalem should now begin. He then traveled on to Amsterdam, where he was able to meet with Jewish leaders, discuss the prophecies about the gathering of the Jews, and hear the rabbis' point of view.

In Prussia, a land that is now part of Germany, he was delayed for a week because he needed a visa to pass through Austria. He decided to put his time to good use by learning German—in one week!

Elder Orson Hyde

Orson Hyde was a very intelligent man, but he also received great help from the Lord. He learned to read and write German with remarkable speed, and was able to read "one book through, and part of another." He also did some translating and writing in German. This skill would prove to be very important to him later.

Elder Hyde traveled on to Constantinople, a city in Turkey that is now called Istanbul, and then to Jerusalem, arriving October 21, 1841. At that time Jerusalem was little more than a village, but its history was magnificent. This was the ancient fortress city of David and Solomon, and it was the holy city where Jesus Christ and his apostles had taught. It was near the place where Christ later died on the cross. But only about twenty thousand people lived in Jerusalem in 1841, and of those, about seven thousand were Jews.

Before sunup on October 24 Orson Hyde walked to the Mount of Olives, just outside Jerusalem. This was the place where Christ had taught his disciples and prophesied the future, and it was close to the Garden of Gethsemane, where Christ poured out his heart to his Father before his crucifixion.

There, in that holy place, Elder Hyde knelt and prayed. He spoke to the Lord of His covenant with Abraham, Isaac, and Jacob. Even though the descendants of these prophets were scattered across the earth, the Lord had promised that they would be gathered again. This had to happen, according to ancient prophecies, before Christ could return to the earth.

Elder Hyde pleaded with the Lord on behalf of the Jews that their "scattered remnants" throughout the world would be led back to the holy city. He asked that the place might be made fertile and "abundantly fruitful" so that it could be lived in. He blessed the Jews that they might come, in time, to believe in Jesus Christ. Elder Hyde then stacked up a pile of stones, a marker for the place where he had offered his prayer of dedication.

Elder Hyde had traveled thousands of miles to get to this place, and he had followed his vision. He had now been gone from his family for a year and a half, without once having the chance to hear from his wife. But he did not rush home. He traveled back to Germany to publish materials about the Church in the language he had taught himself while there before. And he endured a terrible storm at sea, the ship barely staying afloat. He did not reach his home until December 1842. He had been gone more than two-and-a-half years, and he had traveled over twenty thousand miles.

But in the coming years, he began to see the spirit of gathering take hold. At first only a few Jews returned to Jerusalem, but with every passing year the flow increased. By the end of the century, fifty thousand Jews had immigrated to the city. Today, over four million people live in Jerusalem, the vast majority of them Jewish. Ancient prophecies are being fulfilled, and Elder Hyde's vision of the fertile, inviting Jerusalem is now a reality.

For further reading, see Howard H. Barron, *Orson Hyde: Missionary, Apostle, Colonizer* (Bountiful, Utah: Horizon Publishers, 1977).

5

DAN JONES IN WALES

One of the greatest missionaries of the early Church was a little man named Dan Jones—Captain Dan Jones. As a teenager, he left his home in Wales and became a sailor. He immigrated to America in 1840, and at the age of thirty he became captain of his own riverboat on the Mississippi. He prospered, in spite of losing one boat to the hazards of river travel, and he was able to buy half interest in the *Maid of Iowa,* a large vessel that could carry three hundred passengers.

In the early 1840s, as Captain Jones traveled up and down the river from New Orleans to St. Louis, he heard about the Mormons who had settled in Nauvoo, Illinois. Several of their missionary pamphlets came into his hands, and he also had a chance to meet Hyrum Smith and receive a copy of the Book of Mormon. Most of what he heard on the river about Mormons was negative, but Dan Jones liked to make up his own mind. He listened and learned, and in 1843 he was baptized.

When Captain Jones joined the Church, his business fell off badly. People who knew he was a Mormon often refused to travel with him. But Joseph Smith bought half interest in the *Maid of Iowa,* and after that, much of Dan Jones's business was in carrying the Saints up the river to Nauvoo. At the same time, he and Joseph became fast friends. In fact, on the night before Joseph and Hyrum Smith were murdered, Dan Jones was in the Carthage Jail. He had gone there to support and protect the Prophet even though he hadn't been arrested himself.

After the other men in the room had gone to sleep that night, Dan Jones and Joseph Smith talked about the future. They knew that the mob outside might turn violent. "Are you afraid?" Joseph asked Brother Jones. But the captain answered, "Engaged in such a cause, I do not think that death would have many terrors." It was not, however, his time to die. Joseph told him, "You will yet see Wales and fulfill the mission appointed you."

That was the last prophecy Joseph Smith would pronounce. The next morning he asked Dan Jones to carry a letter to a lawyer in Quincy, Illinois. As Captain Jones tried to leave the jail, he was surrounded by the mob, but the little man quickly jumped on his horse. As he rode away, the men began to shoot at him. He ducked against his horse, and bullets whizzed past him. As Joseph had promised, Dan Jones's life was saved. Later that day, however, he learned that his beloved friend and prophet had been shot to death.

The Church did not fall apart as enemies predicted. In fact, Dan Jones was a perfect example of how missionary work increased. That same year, 1844, he returned to Wales as a mission president, just as the Prophet had said he would. And he spent eight of the next eleven years serving in his homeland. When he arrived in Wales, the Church could claim only about three hundred members. But Elder Jones brought an enthusiasm to the work that fired the faith of the handful of missionaries who served with him.

A year later Wales had five hundred members, and at the end of his first mission, which lasted three years, Elder Jones reported to Church leaders that a great conference had been held. He described the attendance: "Our hall, which will hold two thousand people, was so crowded before the morning service commenced that we had to engage another hall nearly as large, which was also soon filled to overflowing, and continued so for two days with but little intermission."

There were now 3,603 members in Wales, 1,939 having been baptized in the previous year. Elder Jones was able to report an average of nearly 1,000 converts per year since he had been in Wales, "with brighter prospects in the future."

The little captain was a great teacher, but he was also a fighter. When attacked in publications by local ministers, he responded with his own pamphlets and fliers—and he held nothing back. Whether he was writing for the Saints in a Welsh-language magazine called the *Prophet of the Jubilee*, or whether he was responding to evil accusations, he fired back directly and he created great controversy. He kept the Welsh people, especially in southern Wales, constantly talking about the "Mormon question." Many hated him and his church, but interest was high, and that caused others to listen and accept the gospel. In fact, one out of every 278 people in Wales joined the Church!

Elder Jones loved to stir up a community by sending out fliers announcing that he would soon preach there—and that his intent was to convert everyone in town. This would enrage the local people, but they would come out to listen. Inevitably, some would have their hearts changed by his sermons. And what sermons they were. Once he preached for seven-and-a-half hours!

On one occasion a blind man named Daniel Jones (a very common name in Wales) came to Dan Jones and asked to be baptized. He also asked Elder Jones to restore his sight. But Elder Jones smelled a Judas—someone who wanted to join the Church only to turn on it and spread false rumors. He told Daniel Jones that he could be baptized and blessed but that the healing would depend on the man's own faith.

Elder Jones's instinct was right; the blind man had mischief in mind. At the time he was administered to, he claimed that he was beginning to see already. But shortly afterward he published a nasty pamphlet full of lies about the incident. In the pamphlet was an anti-Mormon ballad that actually became a popular song in that region of Wales. Dan Jones, however, was not one to run from such a confrontation. He published a persuasive pamphlet of his own which denied the false charges and included statements from eyewitnesses as to what had actually happened. The pot was kept stirring, and more people listened and then joined the Church.

Dan Jones also confronted the blind man personally. He told him that he had lied and that he would pay for his deception. His fate would be hotter than that of Kora, Dathan, and Abiram—three men who were swallowed up in the earth after opposing Moses in the Old Testament.

A short time later, Dan Jones learned that his prediction had come true. Daniel Jones had come down with a fever so intense that his friends had to pour cold water on him night and day. But nothing helped, and the man soon died.

Elder Jones returned to Wales many times, and he brought many of the Welsh Saints to America and across the plains to Salt Lake City and on to other communities. Many settled in southern Idaho. Welsh names are common in the modern Church, and many of the descendants of those early Welsh settlers have become missionaries themselves. Even the Mormon Tabernacle Choir is the out-growth of an early Welsh singing group.

One familiar Welsh name, almost as common as Jones, is Hughes. We—Dean and Tom Hughes—have Dan Jones to thank that our ancestors joined the Church and passed on to us a great heritage.

For further reading, see Gordon B. Hinckley, "The Thing of Most Worth," *Ensign*, September 1993, pp. 2–7; Dan Jones, *Prophet of the Jubilee*, trans. Ronald D. Dennis (Provo, Utah: Ronald D. Dennis, 1981); and Ivan J. Barrett, *Dan Jones* (Salt Lake City: Hawkes Publishing Co., 1989).

6

The First Mission to Sweden

The apostle Paul was whipped five times, beaten by rods three times, stoned once, and was chased and abused throughout all his missions. He suffered hunger and thirst, cold and weariness—and several times he was cast into prison. But he never stopped preaching. These days, most missionaries suffer far less. But in the history of the restored Church, many missionaries have had to put up with harassment and abuse.

One missionary who faced plenty of hardship for the Lord was Elder John E. Forsgren, the first missionary to Sweden. He was called with Elder Erastus Snow (one of the Twelve) and Elder Peter O. Hansen to begin preaching the gospel in the Scandinavian countries—Denmark, Finland, Norway, and Sweden. In England the three were joined by Elder George P. Dykes, and all four arrived in Denmark in the summer of 1850.

Elder Forsgren stayed only a few days in Denmark before he continued on alone to the country of his birth, Sweden. He had been gone from Sweden for twenty years, and so he made his first visit to his brother and sister in the town of Gefle. He found his brother, Peter, gravely ill with consumption—what we now call tuberculosis. Doctors told Elder Forsgren that there was no hope for his brother. He would soon die.

Elder Forsgren, a man of faith, refused to accept that. He laid his hands on his brother's head and healed him by the power of the priesthood. Peter was impressed by this great power and by the truths of the gospel as explained to him by his brother. He was soon baptized, and then his sister, Christina, also joined the Church. They were the first two converts in Sweden.

Elder Forsgren decided to travel on to Stockholm, where he thought more people might be receptive to his message. But before he could leave Gefle, he learned of a group of farmers who were about to board a ship that would leave in just a few days. The people had decided to emigrate to America, where they hoped to find religious freedom. In Sweden, it was illegal to preach anything that was opposed to the Lutheran Church. A person who was brazen enough to preach other doctrines could be arrested.

Elder Forsgren didn't worry about his own safety. These emigrants wanted to hear his message, and so he taught them. In a short time, Elder Forsgren baptized seventeen of them.

On the day after the baptism, Elder Forsgren met with the new members, ordained some of the men to the priesthood, and began to organize them into a branch of the Church. But before the meeting could end, a number of Lutheran priests showed up with policemen. Elder Forsgren was arrested.

The police accused Elder Forsgren of healing the sick. He couldn't—nor did he want to—deny that. Peter Forsgren was called in, and when he witnessed that his brother had indeed healed him, the priests claimed that Peter was mentally ill. A doctor was then called on to examine Peter, but the doctor found that Peter "knew what he was about." The judge was perplexed. Elder Forsgren seemed a decent man, well dressed and in possession of the correct passport and papers from his country.

Finally, the judge decided to do what judges since the time of Christ and Paul have often done. He passed the decision on to someone else. He had Elder Forsgren shipped out of Gefle and on to Stockholm. There, Elder Forsgren testified in front of the highest government officials in the kingdom of Sweden. No one could find him guilty of anything except preaching. Finally, they decided that the best thing to do was to get rid of him by sending him back to America.

While Elder Forsgren was waiting for a ship, the local newspapers printed all sorts of lies about him and the principles he taught. And what effect did this have? Many people sought him out, eager to hear what he really did have to say. For a month he was kept busy, daily teaching the gospel to those who invited him into their homes.

When authorities learned that several people were about to be baptized in spite of the law, they decided they had better get rid of Elder Forsgren immediately. They arrested him again and put him on a ship that would leave the next morning for New York City.

The only problem was that the ship had to stop briefly at Elsinore, a port in Denmark. By then, Elder Forsgren had become friends with the captain of the ship. The captain ignored the wishes of the Swedish government and let his "prisoner" get off the ship in Denmark, where Elder Forsgren could join the other missionaries, who were still in Copenhagen.

The Swedish police had foreseen this possibility, however. They contacted the Danish police, who quickly arrested Elder Forsgren again. They were about to put him back on the ship and send him on to America when a friend of the missionaries, the American ambassador to Denmark, happened to come by and see what was happening.

The ambassador told the police he would take responsibility for the elder. He knew the Mormon missionaries to be trustworthy people. There was nothing the police could do. Elder Forsgren was released and was soon united with Elders Snow, Hansen, and Dykes. The first Swedish mission had not lasted long, but the work would go on in the Scandinavian countries. Eventually thousands of people would come into the Church, many of them in Sweden.

For further reading, see Andrew Jenson, *History of the Scandinavian Mission* (Salt Lake City: Deseret News Press, 1927).

7

B. H. Roberts's First Mission

The first time Brigham H. Roberts was offered the chance to serve a mission, he turned it down. He was a young married man, just out of college. He was teaching school in Centerville, Utah, and he was trying to get enough money together to buy some land so he could start building a home for his family.

At a special meeting, B. H. Roberts's priesthood leader called for volunteers. Missionaries were needed. Brother Roberts believed in missionary work, but he didn't feel he was in a position to go. Others must have felt the same way, because no one volunteered. Finally the leader changed the question: How many would *like* to go if it were possible? To that, Brother Roberts answered yes. He would love to go if he could—but right now he couldn't.

Somehow the word got back to Church leaders in Salt Lake City that he had volunteered. And the next thing Brother Roberts knew, he was on the list of those to be called on missions at the spring conference of 1880. Brother Roberts was quick to get a letter off, telling the General Authorities he was sorry and setting the record straight. In response, his mission was cancelled, and Brother Roberts bought a piece of land and began to dig a basement—by hand. But about that time he got a letter calling him to repentance for not being willing to serve a mission. This was too much for him. He decided to accept a call after all.

By now, his bishop intervened and managed to get the call canceled all over again. No sooner had that happened, however, than President John Taylor called the bishop to Salt Lake City. He wanted to know what the problem was with "young Roberts" that he didn't want to go on a mission. The bishop explained the situation. "Well, Bishop," President Taylor said, "what do you suppose we have bishops in the Church for? If the young man could not maintain his family during his absence, why don't you undertake the job and assure him that they shall not want?"

So B. H. Roberts was called once again—to the Northern States Mission—and that spring he boarded a train for the midwest. He was asked to establish missionary work in the area of Sioux City, Iowa. An experienced missionary, William Palmer, would remain a few days with him in the area, and then, at least for a time, Elder Roberts would be on his own.

The two missionaries got off a train in Omaha, Nebraska, and immediately had a chance to teach a group of investigators who were already being taught by other missionaries. Elder Palmer, a man of considerable experience, spoke to the group first. He preached on and on about a complicated gospel theory he had developed, but those in the audience were not impressed.

When B. H. Roberts was called on to speak, it was his first chance ever to preach the gospel to people outside the Church. He was frightened and confused. But when he arose to speak, he thought of Joseph Smith's first vision and the events that followed. Elder Roberts gave the account simply and directly, then bore his testimony. He felt a response from the Spirit, and he continued to preach. On the following morning, six of the people in the meeting asked for baptism. Elder Roberts began to understand why the Lord had wanted him to fill a mission.

During Elder Roberts's time in Iowa, he had many great experiences that taught him to accept the will of the Lord. After staying for a time with a family named Slade in the Sioux City area, he decided to move on to nearby Mason City. The Slades gave him a little money to get him started.

On the morning he was to leave, Elder Roberts awoke and looked down at the carpet near his bed. He saw two bare feet. Slowly he looked up and saw a beautiful young man, clean shaven, with wavy hair. He was a noble young man, "erect, but not stiff." Elder Roberts was frightened for a moment, but then he relaxed as he felt a wonderful sense of security come over him. The man bent forward and said, in a tender voice, "You are called to go to Rockford."

Instantly the vision ended, and the young man vanished.

Elder Roberts was astounded. He had never experienced anything like this. It took him a moment to accept what he had seen, but then he got out of bed and asked the Slades whether they had ever heard of a place called Rockford. The

Slades didn't recognize the name, but Elder Roberts soon learned that such a little town did exist. And now he had to make a decision.

Elder Roberts was scheduled to go to Mason City, had made all the arrangements, and was embarrassed to seem inconsistent to the Slades. So he decided to go on to Mason City in spite of what had just happened. He could go to Rockford later.

The next few days, however, were a trial. No one in Mason City would take him in, nor could he find a place to preach. On the second night, after a long day with very little to eat, he lay down in an open prairie where he fought with spiders and bugs all night and slept very little. When he sat up the next morning, he whispered to himself, "Well, this is a pretty hard way . . . to serve the Lord!" At that moment, a voice spoke. He saw no one, but he heard the words very clearly: "You were told to go to Rockford." Elder Roberts jumped to his feet and answered the voice: "So I was, and to Rockford I will go!"

Elder Roberts returned immediately to the Slade household. There he was met by a young man named Hyrum Jensen, who had been assigned to serve as his companion. The two wasted no time in heading for Rockford, but they had to walk all the way, a trip that took them a few days. As they approached the city, they intended to stop at farmhouses outside of town to ask for lodging. But each time the two missionaries passed a farm, one or the other would say, "No, not here," and they ended up arriving in town without a place to stay. Elder Roberts was disgusted with himself and his companion. He told Elder Jensen that they seemed to want someone to come out on the sidewalk and ask them in. And he added, "Then I doubt very much if we would have sense enough to go with them."

Shortly after that, a man greeted them and asked where they had come from. Elder Roberts told him that they were missionaries. The man wondered where they planned to stay. The elders explained that they didn't know, that they traveled without money and needed to find someone who would take them in. The man informed them that he owned a hotel. He pointed to it and said, "Go there and put up." And then he walked away.

The elders wondered. Would he let them run up a bill and then try to charge them for the stay? The two continued to consider for a time, and then Elder

Roberts began to laugh. "Hyrum," he said, "it's happened, I tell you; it's happened. . . . Someone has come out on the sidewalk, stopped us, invited us to lodgings, and here we stand discussing whether we had better accept it or not. I told you not five minutes ago that if anyone [did that] I doubt if we had sense enough to accept the offer."

And so the elders found lodging. And this first experience was a sign of good things to come. The two preached to many people in Rockford. They were able to set up regular meetings every week in the local school houses, and eventually they established a branch of the Church. Elder Roberts was able to see very clearly why the Lord had sent him to Rockford.

As winter came on, the cold weather had such an effect on Elder Roberts's health that he was transferred to the Southern States Mission, where it was warmer. He would complete a great mission there. And after returning to his wife, who was cared for as promised while he was gone, he would be home only two years before being called to return to the Southern States Mission as the acting president.

And that would be the mere beginning of B. H. Roberts's service to the Church. He later served many missions and eventually became a General Authority, serving in the First Council of the Seventy. He wrote an extensive work titled *A Comprehensive History of the Church* and many other important publications on Mormonism. He came to be known as the "defender of the faith" for his important service and writings in defense of the Church and its doctrines.

But one wonders. Suppose he had turned down that first mission, as he had plenty of reasons to do. Or suppose his wife, instead of supporting the call, had insisted that he not leave her. Suppose he had missed the great experiences. How differently might his life have turned out?

For further reading, see Robert H. Malan, *B. H. Roberts: A Biography* (Salt Lake City: Deseret Book Co., 1966); Truman G. Madsen, *Defender of the Faith: The B. H. Roberts Story* (Salt Lake City: Bookcraft, 1980); and B. H. Roberts, *The Autobiography of B. H. Roberts* (Salt Lake City: Signature Books, 1990).

8

OLIVER COWDERY'S COURTROOM TESTIMONY

Elder C. M. Nielsen was traveling alone through eastern Minnesota in 1884, preaching the gospel. One morning he walked into a town where he knew no one. He had no food or money, so he was trying to find someone who would offer him some help.

As he neared a store, the Spirit told him to walk over and see a certain man. But he didn't know which man. He recorded what happened next: "One man seemed to me as big as three ordinary men. The Spirit whispered: 'Go over and speak to him!' I hesitated to approach this entire stranger, but the same voice came to me a second and a third time. Then I went."

Elder Nielsen later learned that the man was a wealthy farmer who was very important in the city and in the state of Minnesota, where he had been elected to public offices. But on their first meeting, the conversation went this way:

> Not knowing what else to say, I said: "How far are you going?" "Home; where are you going?" "I have no certain place, I am from Utah." "You are not a Mormon, are you?" he asked, anxiously. "Yes." "Then God bless you!" he replied, reaching out his arms and dropping the lines. "Get into this buggy as fast as you can. When we get home, my wife will rejoice as I rejoice now; I will then explain all. But you are not one of these make-believers, are you?" "No, I'm a real live Mormon."

Elder Nielsen was welcomed and fed by the man's wife, and then the whole family gathered around the table. The man began to explain himself. He told about a strange experience he had had as a young man while living on his father's farm in Michigan. He said that one day he wanted a day off from his farm work, so he rode into the nearest town. He saw that something interesting was going on at the local courthouse, so he walked in and then pushed his way to the front of the courtroom. He discovered that a murder trial was under way.

At that moment, the prosecuting attorney was addressing the jury. He was a man named Oliver Cowdery.

What the young man didn't know was that Oliver Cowdery had been very important to the Prophet Joseph Smith. In fact, he had served as a scribe while Joseph translated the Book of Mormon from the golden plates. He and Joseph had received the Aaronic Priesthood from John the Baptist, who had returned to the earth to assist in the restoration of the gospel. It was Oliver Cowdery who had baptized Joseph after Joseph had baptized him. They had also received the Melchizedek Priesthood together from Peter, James, and John. Perhaps most important, Oliver Cowdery had been chosen by God as one of the men who were allowed to see the angel Moroni with the golden plates, there-

Oliver Cowdery

after to serve as one of the Three Witnesses to the truthfulness of the Book of Mormon.

Later, however, Oliver Cowdery had quarreled with some of the leaders of the Church and had separated himself from the membership. He had become a lawyer, working in Ohio, Wisconsin, and Michigan, and now he was serving as prosecutor in this murder trial. Most people in the area knew nothing of his past connection with the Mormon church.

The prosecutor's background was also unknown to the young man who had pushed his way to the front of the courtroom. He was taken by surprise when the defense attorney got up to speak. The lawyer said nothing about the man charged with murder. Instead, he began to attack Oliver Cowdery: "May it please the court and gentlemen of the jury, I see one Oliver Cowdery is going to reply to my argument. I wish he would tell us something about that golden Bible that Joe Smith dug out of the hill; something about the great fraud he perpetrated upon the American people."

By the time Oliver Cowdery got up to present his own arguments, everyone in the room was wondering what he would say to separate himself from the Mormon church. The defense attorney had attempted to make a fool of him. Would he deny everything, or would he express his regrets for having had anything to do with Joseph Smith?

But Oliver Cowdery denied nothing. Nor did he apologize. In fact, he told the judge and the jury:

> Before God and man I dare not deny what I have said, and what my testimony contains as written and printed on the front page of the Book of Mormon. May it please your honor and gentlemen of the jury, this I say: I saw the angel and heard his voice—how can I deny it? It happened in the daytime when the sun was shining bright . . . ; not in the night when I was asleep. That glorious messenger from heaven . . . told us if we denied that testimony there is no forgiveness in this life nor in the world to come. Now how can I deny it—I dare not; I will not!

The young man standing in the courtroom, hearing this testimony from Oliver Cowdery, was impressed and touched by the Spirit. He believed what he heard. Now, many years later, he had finally met a missionary from the Mormon church, as he had long hoped to do. He told Elder Nielsen: "Since I heard Oliver Cowdery speak, I have not had peace for these many years. I want to know more about your people. . . . If you can show us that you have what Oliver Cowdery testified to, we shall all be glad to receive it."

By this time Oliver Cowdery was dead, but before his death he had returned to the Church. He had gone to his grave regretting the years he had spent away, and especially the opportunities he had lost to serve and lead in the Church. But even during his years of separation, he had never denied his testimony of the Book of Mormon. And on that one occasion in the courtroom, he had served as a missionary—though he had no idea he was doing so. The young man who had wandered into the courtroom that day had never forgotten his stirring words, and years later Elder Nielsen was guided to him so that he could hear the gospel.

In 1884 Elder Nielsen became Oliver Cowdery's missionary companion, even though the two had never met.

This chapter is based on a manuscript by C. M. Nielsen in the Archives of The Church of Jesus Christ of Latter-day Saints, Salt Lake City; as published in Preston Nibley, comp., *Missionary Experiences* (Salt Lake City: Deseret News Press, 1954).

9

The Tennessee Massacre

In 1884, two elders, John Gibbs and William Jones, were assigned by their acting mission president, B. H. Roberts, to visit towns all over Tennessee. Their purpose was to correct false impressions and outright lies being spread about the Church. The elders suffered plenty of abuse along the way, but in August they finally enjoyed rest from their travels. They joined two other missionaries, Elders William Berry and Henry Thompson, at a little settlement on Kane Creek. The missionaries held a baptism for two new members, and then, on the following Sunday, they planned to hold church services in the home of a family named Condor. Enemies had burned down the little church that members of the Kane Creek Branch had previously used.

Before church services began that Sunday, Brother Condor was standing outside when a group of about twenty men came out of the woods and grabbed him. His son Martin and his stepson, James Hudson, could have saved themselves, but Brother Condor shouted to them to run to the house and protect the elders—the obvious target of the mob.

Martin Condor ran into the house just as David Hinson, leader of the mob, tried to pull a shotgun down from the wall. When Martin tried to stop him, Hinson pulled out a pistol and shot at Martin, but the gun misfired. Martin stepped back in reaction, and Hinson used the moment to fire the shotgun at Elder Gibbs. Elder Gibbs was hit just under the arm. He fell to the floor.

At the same moment, when another man aimed a gun at Elder Thompson, Elder Berry grabbed at the gun. Hinson turned and shot Elder Berry. In the confusion, Elder Thompson was able to run out the door. But Martin Condor went after David Hinson and was shot several times by other members of the mob.

About then, Brother Condor's stepson climbed out of the loft, where he had gone to find his own gun. He saw his half brother fall and tried to come to his aid. Two men took hold of him, but he fought his way free and shot Hinson. From outside, other men were firing through the window. One of them shot Sister Condor in the hip.

Everything happened in just a few seconds. Suddenly it was over, and the mob picked up Hinson and cleared out. Four of the Mormons were dead: Elders Berry and Gibbs, Martin Condor, and James Hudson. Melinda Condor was badly hurt but not in danger of dying.

What followed was a scary standoff. The Mormons built wooden coffins and buried their dead in the Condors' yard. Members of the mob set up guards and vowed not to let any Mormons come in to take away the elders' bodies. And wild rumors spread throughout the region. Some accounts claimed that all the Mormons in the branch and all the missionaries had been murdered.

Another missionary, Willis Robison, heard the rumors and decided that he had to get to Kane Creek and find out what really had happened and what he could do. He set out in spite of warnings that he would be killed if he tried to get to the Condors' house.

Elder Robison took a train part of the way and then walked thirty miles. As he neared the Condor home, two hard-looking men met him at a train trestle. Elder Robison had dressed in work clothes, and he tried to sound like

President B. H. Roberts in disguise

a rough character. When asked where he was going, he said he was looking for work picking cotton. But the men were suspicious. They crossed the trestle with him, one in front and one behind. Elder Robison was ready for anything. He vowed to himself that if they tried to throw him off the trestle, he would take at least one of them with him.

But Elder Robison's rude style calmed the men's suspicions; they decided to let him go. The missionary was able to sneak along creeks and through wooded areas until he reached the Condors' home in the middle of the night. There, he learned that he could now be of no help. He could not move the murdered elders' bodies, and the surviving missionaries had escaped the area safely.

The Condors told him he had better leave before he brought trouble on himself and the other Mormons. So Elder Robison had a bite to eat, and even though he had walked all day and most of the night, he left before sunrise. When he reached the trestle, he had a new problem. The sun was coming up, and people were stirring. Some were hunting in the nearby woods. To reach the trestle he would have to leave the woods and walk past several homes.

He later wrote that as he was thinking about what to do, "one of those heavy river fogs suddenly settled down on the scene before me and seemed almost to have come on purpose for my benefit." He took off his squeaky boots and ran to the trestle. He crossed "double time," without anyone seeing him, even though he could hear people a short distance away. As soon as he reached the woods on the opposite side of the trestle, the fog lifted. Elder Robison walked all day again. His feet became so swollen that he had to cut his boots open so he could keep going. But he made it back to his companion.

One problem still had to be resolved: Elder Gibbs and Elder Berry still lay in shallow graves in Kane Creek, and their parents would want to bury them at home.

By now, President B. H. Roberts had gotten the bad news. For a young man still in his twenties, he was faced with a huge responsibility. He felt that he must somehow get the bodies of the elders home to their parents. He was told that he would be going to his death should he try to enter Kane Creek, but he heard a voice say, "You will go to secure those bodies and all will be well with you, but you must go."

A young man named J. Golden Kimball, who would also serve the Church as a General Authority one day, was the mission secretary. President Roberts put him in charge of arranging transportation for the elders' bodies and then, with two wagons and the help of two young men, set out for Kane Creek.

President Roberts used a disguise as Elder Robison had done. He dressed as a stable worker, and he cut his nicely trimmed beard to a rough stubble. He added some dirt and a slouchy hat, and he looked like anything but the refined, educated man he was.

As it turned out, President Roberts arrived in Kane Creek as the surveillance by the mob was lifting. He was able to ride in, dig up the bodies, and get back on his way before anyone knew what had happened. The great difficulty for him was that he wanted to throw off his disguise and go bless Sister Condor and comfort the other Saints. He knew he couldn't do that, however, and so he continued quickly on his way.

On the way back, President Roberts got confused. At a fork in the road, he stayed left when he should have gone right. The mistake, though it added twelve miles to his trip, was a blessing. Some of the local enemies of the Church had learned that the bodies were being removed, and they had chased after the wagons. These enemies were lying in wait on the right fork of the road.

Elder Robison, who had tried to reach the missionaries in their time of need, was nearing the end of his mission, and so he was released to take the bodies back to Utah. He wondered why he had been protected when others had made the ultimate sacrifice, giving their lives. But Elders John Gibbs and William Perry, along with Martin Condor and James Hudson, had entered royal company. These men had joined the ranks of such martyrs as Joseph and Hyrum Smith and Parley P. Pratt. They had sealed their testimonies with their own blood.

For further reading, see Truman G. Madsen, *Defender of the Faith: The B. H. Roberts Story* (Salt Lake City: Bookcraft, 1980); and Willis Robison, "Mission Journal," MSS 799, Special Collections, Brigham Young University Library.

10

WITHOUT PURSE OR SCRIP

Today, in most cases, missionaries begin their service at a missionary training center. When they reach their field of labor, they are guided by experienced senior companions. These modern missionaries usually think they live in humble circumstances, but if their rooms are not fancy, at least they do have places to live. And each month a check arrives, even if it is rather small.

The earliest Mormon missionaries, however, carried no money with them. This was called preaching "without purse or scrip." *Scrip* is a word we don't use much anymore, but it refers to paper money.

This method of preaching the gospel continued into the early part of the twentieth century. The stories of how missionaries got by without purse or scrip are inspiring, amazing, and sometimes even funny. One such missionary was a young man from North Ogden, Utah, named David Crockett Shupe. He left on his mission to the Southern States in the fall of 1898, when he was twenty-two. He traveled by train to Tennessee, where he was introduced to his first companion, Elder Duffin.

Elder Shupe soon learned the life of a traveling missionary. Each day he and his companion tramped through the hills and valleys of Tennessee and stopped at farms and villages to knock on doors and hand out pamphlets or "tracts." Sometimes they would get permission to use a school or a church, and then they would try to attract people to attend a meeting and hear them teach the gospel.

Every day the missionaries also had to obtain enough to eat, and every night they had to find a place to sleep. Elder Shupe had begun his mission with $33.00 in his pocket, so he had a little money to fall back on. But it was soon gone. Thus when he and his companion knocked on people's doors, they not only asked to come in and preach but also requested dinner and a bed.

These were different times, of course, and when a minister of the gospel asked for a place to stay, many people would open their doors. However, by the turn of the century, all sorts of rumors and lies about Mormon doctrine had been circulated in the southern United States. Many people, on learning which church the missionaries came from, would not take them in. In some cases they would even spread the word through the area to drive the elders away.

A typical day in the lives of Elder Shupe and Elder Duffin might involve a walk of maybe three to twelve miles, rejection at many doors, then finally the discovery of a family who would listen and who would take them in. Or sometimes they could find a hotel keeper who would take pity on them and put them up for free.

But those were the good days. Elder Shupe's journal, in which he recorded every day of his mission, tells about all the other kinds of days as well. Being out in the weather all winter meant days when he and his companions slogged through muck, ankle deep, and arrived at homes in shoes that were caked with thick mud. Often the young men would cross rivers with their shoes off and their trousers rolled up, but on one occasion Elder Shupe's companion tried to jump a river and didn't make it. So Elder Shupe decided to cross on a tree limb—and fell off. The two spent the afternoon on the banks of the river drying their clothes—not only the ones on their backs, but their change of clothes that they carried in "grips" or carpet bags.

Sickness was a constant problem. Not only did the elders suffer from illnesses, but they also endured rashes, mosquito and tick bites, headaches, blistered feet, fevers, and boils. During one period of time, Elder Shupe suffered with a toothache and had no opportunity to see a dentist. Summers in Tennessee were hot and humid, winters rainy and muddy. Roads were bad, and there were snake-infested swamps that had to be crossed. Sometimes the elders kept going only because of their faith and their priesthood power, which they used to heal each other.

The missionaries rarely had to go without more than a meal or two at a time, but sometimes they had themselves an extra "fast day," whether they planned it that way or not. And just as bad, sometimes they found no place to sleep and had to make do in the woods or in a barn. When Elder Shupe had a chance to take a real bath, not in a river but in a bathtub, he would record that special event in his diary. It wasn't something that happened very often.

Occasionally the elders did receive additional help. One day, Elder Shupe was able to get to a post office where he received a package from home. In the package were seven dollars, a pair of long underwear, and an umbrella. That was a happy day!

Shortly after Elder Shupe began his mission, he received word that his father had died. It was one of the worst days of his life. By the time he got the letter, the funeral was over. Elder Shupe sat for a time and tried to find comfort in knowing that he was doing God's work, and then he and Elder Duffin walked several miles before they got a chance to preach. They entered into a good conversation, but the man of the family became angry and threw the elders out. They had to keep going until they found a family who would take them in for the night. And when they finally did, Elder Shupe was thankful to have a place to rest. His father was still very much on his mind.

Elder Shupe often wrote in his diary about harassment from Christian ministers. Typically, when the elders set up a meeting, the local preachers would disrupt the sermons with unfriendly questions and accusations. But through it all the elders kept their patience, sang the songs of Zion, preached the doctrine, and more often than not moved on with little sense that anyone had taken their message to heart.

Throughout his mission, however, Elder Shupe kept his good spirit and even a sense of humor. After one particularly terrible night, he recorded in his journal the reason for his misery. "It is very hard to describe the loneliness that a Mormon elder experiences at times," he began, but then he said: "My sleep was broken up entirely with the insidious flea crawling on [one] part of my body to another. Following that came the clumsy tick, which occasionally burr[owed] himself beneath the surface of my skin, and the little redheaded impetuous chigger biting here and there, and the lonely bed bug joined in the circle and assisted with the frolicsome tricks upon [my] vanquished form." He added that he couldn't sleep the next night either—because of all the bites. These passages are as close as his journal ever gets to self-pity, and even then he has fun with his descriptions.

One thing Elder Shupe rarely mentioned was a baptism. On one occasion, just before he was transferred from Tennessee, he did mention a woman who was a "candidate for baptism," but then he explained that her sons had talked her out of going through with it. Missionaries at that time often preached and moved on, then returned to the area later to follow up with those who were interested. But they never knew all the seeds they had planted, so it was not uncommon for a later missionary to see the fruits of the labor. Elder Shupe, however, appears not to have been blessed with such opportunities. He walked on and on, day after day, preached and survived all the hardships—and saw very little in the way of success. Most missionaries find their greatest joy in seeing people embrace the gospel and enter the Church, but Elder Shupe preached and preached, walked and walked, and more than anything else met resistance and rejection.

But late in his mission he was transferred to Virginia, and while there he finally had a chance to perform a baptism. He gathered with a group of members at a river, and after delivering a sermon on baptism he "led one honest soul down in the water."

This was the only time he mentioned such an event in his journal. One is reminded of the scripture: "And if it so be that you should labor all your days in crying repentance unto this people, and bring, save it be one soul unto me, how great shall be your joy with him in the kingdom of my Father!" (D&C 18:15.)

As Elder Shupe's mission drew to a close, he might well have focused on the bed bugs and fleas, the mud and swollen rivers—and the thousands of miles he had walked in every sort of weather. But as missionaries have done throughout the history of the Church, he spoke of his great experiences and all that he had learned. He knew he was a bigger, stronger man, and he knew that he had given his all for the sake of the gospel.

When he arrived in Ogden and got off the train, it was apparent that his mother and family didn't know when he was coming in. No one was there to greet him. So Elder Shupe did what he had done for more than two years. He picked up his grip and began to walk. After all, his home was only a few miles to the north, and the road wasn't bad—just a little muddy.

This chapter is based on David Crockett Shupe, "Mission Diary," MSS 799, Special Collections, Brigham Young University Library.

11

HUGH B. BROWN AT THE BACK DOOR

When he was a young man, Hugh B. Brown served a mission in England. His first assignment, in 1904, was in Cambridge, home of one of the world's most famous universities. His first day there showed little promise. All day he went from door to door by himself, handing out pamphlets and asking for opportunities to teach. He was turned down at every door. The next day went the same way. As he returned home that night, he was discouraged. He was an eager young missionary, and he wasn't used to the idea that most people didn't want to listen to him.

That evening Elder Brown heard a knock at his door. When his landlady opened the door, a man asked for Elder Brown. But the young missionary wasn't so sure this was good news. The last missionaries to work in Cambridge had been ordered out by a mob—at gunpoint. Elder Brown wondered whether the same group might be planning a similar going-away party for him.

But Elder Brown greeted the gentleman—and saw the man's surprise. He apparently expected someone called "Elder" to look a little less like a boy. But the man was holding one of the tracts Elder Brown had been handing out, and what he had to say was rather amazing:

> Elder Brown, last Sunday a group of us in the Church of England left the church because we could not agree with our minister. He was not teaching what we believe to be the gospel. There were seventeen of us heads of families who were out of harmony with the minister, and we told him we would not return. We all assembled in my home. I have a large home with a large, hall-like front room which accommodates us and our families. Will you come tomorrow night and be our pastor?

Elder Brown didn't fall over—but he certainly must have gulped.
The man then added that the new congregation had been praying all week

that they would find a new preacher by Sunday. They were sure the Lord had answered their prayers by sending Elder Brown to them.

Elder Brown answered confidently that he would be happy to preach to the group. But the truth was, he was terrified. This would be his first public sermon since arriving in England, and the responsibility was almost overwhelming. He ate no dinner that night, and he spent the evening praying for God's help. The next morning he got up early but continued to fast. He spent the entire day walking through the streets of Cambridge. How could he answer the needs of these people? What should he say to them?

Elder Hugh B. Brown

As the time for the sermon came closer, he was depressed and worried. He simply didn't feel ready for the great task ahead of him. He wondered why the Lord would put him in such a difficult position so early in his mission. Still, he put on his winter coat and his stiff hat, grabbed his Bible and his walking stick, and tried to look as mature and confi-dent as possible. These people were expecting a pastor, not an inexperienced young man.

When Elder Brown knocked on the door of the house, he was welcomed by the man he had met the day before. "Welcome, reverend sir, come in," the man said. Elder Brown's nervousness took another leap. And then, as he entered the room, everyone stood up out of respect. Elder Brown's heart was suddenly in his throat.

At that point he realized that he was expected to conduct the entire meet-ing—lead the music and say the prayers as well as deliver the sermon. In his con-fusion, he asked the people to begin by singing "O My Father." This was an LDS hymn, and no one else in the room knew it, so no one could join in. Elder Brown's singing was never great, but on this occasion his nerves turned the hymn into a disaster.

Anxious to get all the eyes off him for a moment, Elder Brown then asked the congregation to kneel at their chairs and join him in prayer. As he prayed, he included this petition: "These people are seeking for the truth. We have that truth, but I am not able to give it to them without thy help. Wilt thou take over and speak to these people through thy Holy Spirit and let them know the message of truth."

Elder Brown got to his feet. He spoke for forty-five minutes. His sermon got better as he went along, and he felt his self-assurance grow. When he was finished, the congregation was thrilled. All in attendance knew they had heard the truth they had been searching for. Within three months every single person was baptized—all seventeen families.

Elder Brown now knew that he could preach with authority and power when he relied on the Lord. But never again did he bring such a large group into the Church. He had many discouraging experiences, and he continued to receive rejections from most of the people he tried to teach.

One day he was going door to door in Norwich, England. He knocked on a door and received no answer. Through an open window he saw a woman sitting in her living room, knitting. He knocked again, but she still didn't answer. What he didn't know was that she had spotted him, recognized that he was a Mormon missionary, and decided not to go to the door.

But Elder Brown was not so easily ignored. He wanted her to hear what he had to say. So he walked around her house and knocked hard, with his walking stick, on the back door. Needless to say, the woman flew to her door and gave the missionary quite a talking to. Elder Brown later wrote:

> When she did stop, I said, "My dear lady, I apologize for having annoyed you, but our Heavenly Father sent me 6,000 miles to bring you a message, and inasmuch as he sent me I can't go home until I give you that message."
> "Do you mean the Lord sent a message to me?" she asked.
> "I mean just that," I answered. "He sent me because he loves you."
> "Tell me the message."

After telling her the story of Joseph Smith and the restoration of the gospel to the earth, he apologized again for disturbing her. Then he added, "Sister, when you and I meet again, and we will meet again, you are going to say, 'Thank you, and thank God that you came to my back door and insisted on speaking to me.'"

Ten years later, Hugh Brown was in England again, this time as a soldier in World War I. A conference was scheduled in Norwich, but the mission president was sick and couldn't attend. He called Major Brown to see if he could go fill in. He did so willingly. At the end of the meeting, a woman came up to see him. Tears rolled down her cheeks as she kissed his hand. She said:

> I do thank God that you came to my door ten years ago. When you left that day, I thought about what you had said. I couldn't get it out of my mind. I was fighting it, but I couldn't sleep that night. I kept thinking, 'God has sent a message to me.' . . . I tried to find the missionaries from the address on the tract you left, and when I found them, you had returned to Canada. We continued to investigate until my daughter and I joined the Church.

Elder Brown was deeply touched, and he remembered all the doors he had knocked on during his mission—and all of the rejections. He wondered whether other people he had taught had later accepted the gospel.

Early in Elder Brown's mission he had experienced something rare and inspiring—seventeen families entering the Church together. The Lord had led him to the people, and they had been prepared to accept what he had taught. It was a magnificent spiritual experience. But it was his hard work, devotion, and perseverance that had kept him trying in Norwich. And after ten years, he could see the worth of all that effort. In many ways, this was a more important lesson for a young man to learn—a young man who would eventually become a stake president, a mission president, and an apostle of the Lord.

For further reading, see Eugene E. Campbell and Richard D. Poll, *Hugh B. Brown: His Life and Thought* (Salt Lake City: Bookcraft, 1975); and Hugh B. Brown, *An Abundant Life: The Memoirs of Hugh B. Brown,* ed. Edwin B. Firmage (Salt Lake City: Signature Books, 1988).

12

MATTHEW COWLEY'S FAITH

We usually think of missionaries as teachers, and we consider investigators the students. But sometimes the opposite is true. Missionaries learn from the people they teach. That was certainly true when young Matthew Cowley, seventeen years old, was called to his first mission.

When Matthew received his call, he thought of it as a dream come true. He had been called to Hawaii, where his brother Moses had served. Matthew had always wanted to go there. But then something strange happened. The Cowleys' next door neighbor in Salt Lake City was Anthon H. Lund, a member of the First Presidency of the Church. President Lund told Matthew: "I was having dinner tonight, and the Spirit told me you should go to New Zealand instead of Hawaii. I don't know why. That's the way I feel. If it is all right with you, I will tell President Smith in the morning and you will be sent to New Zealand."

Matthew might well have resisted the change, since his heart was set on Hawaii, but he didn't. He accepted the inspiration of a man he trusted. He could not possibly have known how important the change would be. As it would turn out, Elder Cowley would devote much of his life to the people of New Zealand, whom he would come to love and from whom he would learn a great deal.

Think of going on a mission at age seventeen—to a completely foreign culture and thousands of miles from home. Now think of staying on that mission for five years. That's what Matthew Cowley did. He arrived in New Zealand in the fall of 1914 and didn't return until 1919. He entered the mission field as a boy and returned as a man of God.

The natives of New Zealand are called Maoris. They are a people of powerful, simple faith. And young Elder Cowley learned quickly from the Maori people. It was among them that he acquired the two great spiritual gifts he would use all his life: the gift of tongues and the gift of healing.

The first few weeks of Elder Cowley's mission were hard. The language was confusing, and Elder Cowley was beginning to realize how much he lacked both in his ability to preach and in his knowledge of the gospel. He knew he had to follow the example of the Maoris and use faith to meet his challenges. He later described his learning techniques this way:

Elder Matthew Cowley

> How I remember as a mere boy—I was alone for three months without a companion, not understanding the native language—how I would go into the grove every morning at six o'clock and study for eleven hours and fast and pray. Finally, within eleven or twelve weeks and all by myself with no missionary to encourage me, I had the audacity to stand up before a group of natives and preach the gospel in their own tongue. I was using words I had never read or heard, and there was a burning in my bosom the like of which I have never felt before nor since in my life. . . . The power of God was speaking through me as a youngster, seventeen years of age.

From that day on, he spoke to the Maoris only in their own language. And his skill with the language became well known. One of the reasons he remained in New Zealand so long was that his mission president asked him to stay and translate the Book of Mormon, then the Doctrine and Covenants, and finally the Pearl of Great Price.

Elder Cowley learned that translation required more than knowledge. In a letter to his sister, he explained how he did the work:

The work [of translating] was extremely interesting and was comparatively easy when I had the spirit of it. At intervals, however, I would lose the spirit, and this would cause me to spend hours over one short verse. Sometimes I could not work at all.

When I found myself in this predicament I would lock myself in my room, fast and pray, until I felt the urge to continue. . . . Now when I read these books, I marvel that I was the one that was supposed to have done the translating. The language surpasses my own individual knowledge of it. This was the great experience of my life, and it will always remind me that God can and will accomplish his purposes through the human mind.

But how had such a young man acquired this kind of faith? Perhaps it seemed only natural among the Maori people. One day, shortly after arriving in the mission field, a woman ran to him and told him her son had fallen from a tree and was badly hurt. Elder Cowley followed her home, but when he saw the boy, very seriously injured, he told her she should call a doctor. "We don't need a doctor," the mother told him. "You fix him up."

Elder Cowley had never administered to anyone in his life. He was frightened by the mother's expectations of him. But he knelt down and anointed the boy with consecrated oil, and then sealed the anointing himself and blessed the child. The next day, the boy was not only well; he was climbing trees again.

This was only the first of many miracles Elder Cowley was to see brought about by the faith of the Maori people. He wrote of dozens of similar experiences, and in the accounts one can see how the boy missionary was growing:

I was taken across the bay, and walked through [a] village, and in every home there were cases of typhoid fever. I walked fearlessly, with my head erect, impelled by the priesthood of God which I held, and in each of these homes I left the blessings of heaven, and I laid my hands on the sick. And then I had to go across the bay again and get on my horse and ride all night long to arrive at another native village where there was sickness.

When Matthew Cowley returned to Salt Lake City, he finally began college. He studied law, but he had hardly entered his profession before he was called to return to New Zealand, this time as a mission president. The Maoris often came to him for help. Perhaps the most amazing story is one he told of a young father asking for a "small" favor:

> I was asked to administer to a baby in New Zealand. I was asked to bless it. The father came up to me with this child, fourteen months old, and he said, "Our child has not been blessed yet, so I want you to give it a name." I said, "All right. What is the name?" He gave me the name of the child, and then he said in a matter-of-fact way, "While you are giving it its name, give it its sight." The child was born blind. He said, "We have had it to the specialists in Wellington. They said it was born blind and they cannot do anything for it. So while you are giving it a name, by the same authority you use to give it a name, give it its vision." Just as simple as that!
>
> Well, I was scared. I never had that faith. The thing came to me just suddenly like out of the blue. But I went on and blessed the baby with a name. It was the longest blessing, I think, I have ever given. I was using all the words I could think of and had ever thought of. I was trying to get enough inspiration—enough nerve, if you want to call it that—to bless that child with its vision. I finally did.
>
> Eight months later I saw the child, and the child saw me.

Elder Cowley, after all his great experiences in New Zealand, was still learning faith from the Maoris, as he did all his life. The boy missionary would eventually become an apostle, and he would be known for his great speaking ability and for his amazing faith. And throughout his life he would be assigned to serve the people of the Pacific islands. He would continue to return to the people he loved and the people who loved him.

For further reading, see Henry A. Smith, *Matthew Cowley: Man of Faith* (Salt Lake City: Bookcraft, 1986); and Matthew Cowley, "Among the Polynesians," *Improvement Era*, November 1948, pp. 699, 756–58.

13

MELVIN J. BALLARD AT FORT PECK

Mission presidents are missionaries. They are called to lead and administer, but they also set the pace for their missionaries in teaching and testifying of the truths of the gospel. Many stories can be told of the way mission presidents have carried out that duty. One inspiring account is that of Melvin J. Ballard. For several years he served as president of the Northwestern States Mission. This experience helped prepare him for the call to the apostleship, which would soon come.

In 1913, President Ballard was traveling by train through Montana when, near the town of Poplar, he noticed an encampment of several hundred Native Americans at the Fort Peck Reservation. He wanted to meet with these people, so he got off the train and arranged to stay overnight. He hired a horse and buggy and found an interpreter, and then he drove out to the camp at a place called Chicken Hill.

As President Ballard walked among the people, he received a wonderful welcome which at first he could not understand. But the interpreter told him that many of these Dakota and Sioux Indians had experienced dreams in which a white man came among them with his arms full of books—books of great importance to them. They now recognized President Ballard as that man, and they wanted to know whether he had the books.

The tribes gathered and listened to President Ballard speak. He told them the story of the Book of Mormon and explained its great significance to them. And then he told them that he would return and bring the books. He did return, of course, and he not only brought copies of the Book of Mormon, but he also taught them himself and saw to it that other missionaries were sent. Many of these Native Americans joined the Church, and a branch was established.

While in Poplar, President Ballard took interest in the town, which was just then being established. He bought two building lots there. On one of his return visits, he found that the land had greatly increased in value. He sold the land and gained a good profit. Then he used the money, not for himself but to buy land closer to Chicken Hill, where he established a school and a chapel for the Dakota and Sioux of Fort Peck.

Elder John O. Simonsen, who later served as a missionary to this people, understood the love the Native Americans had for President Ballard. He saw firsthand what had impressed them. President Ballard never considered himself above them, even though they lived in the humblest of circumstances. He would go into their simple tents or shelters, sit on the floor with them, and accept the food they offered.

On one visit, a young boy heard of President Ballard's arrival and asked to be taken to him. The boy had been blind since birth. He asked, in his simple faith, that the "Mormon Prayer Man" bless him with his sight. President Ballard did bless him, and the boy received his sight. Just as Christ had blessed the blind and restored their sight, a modern missionary had done the same. Afterwards, the boy

President Melvin J. Ballard

was known to the tribe by the name of "Looking." He joined the Church, and every year when he cut the hay on his small field, he donated it to the Church for cattle that were kept at Chicken Hill.

This was only one of the miracles that occurred among the tribes at Chicken Hill. The people had great faith, which they used to bless each other. They gave credit to President Ballard, who, as a personal witness of Christ, had taught them the gospel. But President Ballard always gave credit to the Dakota and Sioux, whose belief had increased the power of his own faith.

President Ballard's devotion to the native peoples of the Americas did not end when he left his mission. Years later, as an apostle, he went to South America to begin missionary work there.

In 1851 Elder Parley P. Pratt had tried to begin a mission in South America, but the people were not ready. In 1925, on Christmas Day, Elder Melvin J. Ballard stood in the park of Tres de Febrero in Buenos Aires, Argentina, and dedicated South America for the preaching of the gospel of Jesus Christ. He prayed: "I turn the key, unlock, and open the door for the preaching of the Gospel in all these South American nations, and do rebuke and command to be stayed every power that would oppose the preaching of the Gospel. . . . And we do all this that salvation may come to all men, and that thy name may be honored and glorified in this part of the land of Zion."

The work did not move quickly right away. But the apostle knew that great things were going to happen in South America. He pronounced a great prophecy of what was in store for the Church there: "The work of the Lord will grow slowly for a time here just as an oak grows slowly from an acorn. . . . The day will come when the Lamanites in this land will be given a chance. The South American Mission will be a power in the Church."

Elder Ballard did not live to see how completely this prophecy would be fulfilled, but his grandson, Elder M. Russell Ballard of the Council of the Twelve, did. In fact, he participated in making it happen. In December 1985, sixty years after his grandfather dedicated the continent, Elder Ballard traveled to Lima, Peru, where he rearranged three stakes of the Church into seven. The grandfather had dedicated a continent where only four members of the Church lived—the grandson returned to a continent where there were hundreds of thousands. Now, ten years later, there are more than a million members in South America, and the growth continues at a rapid pace.

For further reading, see *Melvin J. Ballard: Crusader for Righteousness* (Salt Lake City: Bookcraft, 1966); and M. Russell Ballard, "The Kingdom Rolls Forth in South America," *Ensign,* May 1986, pp. 12–15.

14

EVACUATION FROM GERMANY

In August 1939, Hitler began to mass troops along the border of Poland. War was about to begin in Europe. The Church sent out word for all missionaries to leave immediately. Those in eastern Germany were to head to Denmark; those in the western and southern parts of Germany were to escape to Holland.

The nation was in chaos. Trains were being taken over for troops, and telephone lines were jammed. Missionaries were soon on their own, with little chance to communicate with mission leaders.

The missionaries knew they were allowed, by law, to take only ten marks (about two dollars) out of the country. So they bought train tickets and then gave away the rest of their money to members, or bought items they could take with them. That worked fine for those heading to Denmark, and all missionaries from the East German Mission were soon safely out of the country.

Escape into Holland was another matter. Dutch leaders remembered World War I, when they had been unable to feed the thousands of refugees, and thus government officials closed the borders. A few missionaries made it through before the closure, and one sister got across by showing that she had a ticket to travel on to London on a steamer. But most missionaries were stopped.

Without money to buy train tickets, the missionaries couldn't get to any other country. Some managed to get telephone calls through to President M. Douglas Wood of the West German Mission, so he at least knew the problem. But many were stranded, and President Wood had no way to know where all of them were.

That's when miracles began to happen. In Frankfurt, President Wood gave five hundred marks to Elder Norman Seibold. The president told Elder Seibold that thirty-one missionaries were unaccounted for and that he must use his own inspiration to find them, get money or tickets to them, and get them to Denmark. At the same time, President Franklin J. Murdock of the Netherlands

Mission received word that six missionaries were stuck just inside the border of Holland. He sent Elder John Kest to find them and to reassure Dutch officials that the missionaries would be sent on to America.

Elder Seibold was a big man. He had played football for the University of Utah. He also proved to be a man of great faith. He had no idea where to find the missionaries, and so he had to follow his own impressions. When he reached Cologne, Germany, after standing up all night on a crowded train, he got off in the huge, crowded station. He climbed on top of a baggage cart and began to whistle "Do What Is Right." He later said it was a bit of a miracle that anyone recognized the song, since he couldn't "carry a tune in a bushel basket." But eight missionaries did recognize the tune and came out of the crowd.

Unfortunately, the tune also attracted a German policeman. He questioned Elder Seibold and then demanded that he turn over his money. But Elder Seibold had *promised* to get the missionaries out. He looked the policeman in the eye and told him that if he tried to take the money, there would be a fight. In Nazi Germany, no one talked that way to the police. Elder Seibold knew that. But he felt he had no choice.

When the policeman demanded that the missionary come with him to a police station, again Elder Seibold said no. He later wrote: "I told him I would go see the military police, but I would not go into the city at all. Why I did that I don't know, but because I was large maybe the Lord made me look larger or something, and I got away with it." Strangely, the military policeman listened. He even agreed to write a letter that allowed Elder Seibold to carry the money and to leave the nation with the missionaries he was trying to find.

For the next three days Elder Seibold searched along the Dutch/German border. In one little town, he saw no reason to get off the train. But a feeling came over him that he must, and so he followed the voice of the Spirit. The little train station was nearly empty, so Elder Seibold walked into the town and then felt impressed to enter a restaurant. He found two elders who had just spent their last pennies for a glass of apple juice. He gave them tickets and money and sent them on their way to Denmark. Then he got back on the train and continued to search.

Meanwhile, Elder Kest arrived in Oldenzaal, Holland, expecting to find at least six missionaries. What he learned was that the elders had been sent back across the border to Bentheim, Germany. Elder Kest had not expected to cross the border, so he hadn't gotten a visa. The missionaries were only a few kilometers away, but he had no way to reach them.

For a few hours he tried making phone calls to government offices. He hoped to get a visa. But all was chaos, and nothing could be done. So Elder Kest, having been instructed to use his best judgment, took a chance. He used all the money he had with him to buy ten tickets to Copenhagen—in case more than six elders were waiting in Bentheim—and then he boarded the train without a visa. For some reason the Dutch authorities did not check his passport, and the train pulled out.

Elder Kest knew he had gotten over the border by a miracle, but in Germany he faced Gestapo officers who did question him about his visa. Then they took him to a room in the station and searched him. They began confiscating everything in his pockets, and he could see they were going to do the same with the train tickets. On impulse, he pulled the tickets out of his pocket and laid them on the table in front of him.

Then another miracle happened. The tickets sat in front of the officers, in plain view, but no one seemed to see them. The officers took everything else Elder Kest had and then told him he could get the items back when he boarded a return train into Holland. At that point, Elder Kest picked up the tickets and put them back in his pocket. "Not an eye flickered," he later reported. Again, the tickets seemed invisible to the officers.

When Elder Kest left the train station, he had forty minutes until he had to reboard and return to Holland. He had no idea where the missionaries were. But someone told him that some Americans had been seen at a hotel in town. Elder Kest hurried to the hotel and found the missionaries. They had used the last of their money to buy some hard rolls and jam. They had prayed constantly for help, and suddenly, like an angel, Elder Kest was there with tickets to Copenhagen. The group knelt together and thanked the Lord, and then Elder Kest ran to catch his train.

The problems were not over, however. Trains were not guaranteed to run on a set schedule. Troops were being rushed to Poland, and passengers with valid tickets were being bumped. For all of the missionaries, not just those in Bentheim, the next couple of days were crazy.

Missionaries boarded any train heading in the direction they needed to go. Sometimes they would get off and try for something else after traveling only a few kilometers. One group reported changing trains seventeen times—and choosing trains by following their inspiration more than by any sort of logic. In another case, a German soldier gave two elders money for train tickets. Two other elders ran across a track in order to board a departing train, and they were arrested. When they complained to a policeman that others were doing the same thing, he turned to look and the elders ran for it. They jumped on the caboose of a moving train with the help of a conductor, who pulled them up.

Elder Seibold made it to Hamburg with several other missionaries, but the group could find no space on any train. Finally they were allowed, for reasons they didn't understand, to board a troop train heading north. But at the border they were stopped. It was then that Elder Seibold pulled out the letter written by the military policeman in Cologne. And that letter, which he received only because of his own stubbornness, won him and his friends safe passage out of the country.

In all, Elder Seibold had collected seventeen of the thirty-one missing missionaries. The other fourteen had made it out on their own or through the help of Elder Kest. Of the 150 missionaries, every person made it out of the country to safety.

Elder Joseph Fielding Smith of the Quorum of the Twelve had been touring the missions of Europe with his wife at the time. They had managed to get out of Germany to Holland before the border closed and then, amazingly, had gotten a flight to Copenhagen. Elder Smith wanted to be there as the missionaries arrived. He spent the next several weeks arranging for their passage out of Europe. Each day, during the wait, he met with them and taught them principles of the gospel. This turned out to be one of the great experiences of most of these young missionaries' lives. Elder Smith later bore powerful testimony that he knew the Lord had protected His missionaries and led them safely home.

This chapter is based on Ellis T. Rasmussen and John Robert Kest, "Border Incident," *Improvement Era,* December 1943, pp. 752–53, 793–97; Myron Douglas Wood, "Interview," Archives of The Church of Jesus Christ of Latter-day Saints, Salt Lake City; and Norman G. Seibold, "Interview," Archives of The Church of Jesus Christ of Latter-day Saints, Salt Lake City.

15

"I Stay in Kaliki!"

In 1941, a young woman from Salt Lake City named Elizabeth Taylor was called on a mission to the Hawaiian Islands. A special mission had been established to teach the many Japanese Americans who lived in Hawaii. Most of the younger Japanese spoke English, but they were deeply tied to their heritage, and effective missionary work required an understanding of those traditions.

Elizabeth Taylor's diary expresses great commitment to her work—and a wonderful, innocent enthusiasm. She loved the people she taught, and her attitude was always upbeat. A typical entry in her journal would read: "Visited 29 homes and were invited into seven homes. Had good discussions in each home. Delivered and explained 14 tracts. All were friendly—gave grand feeling that we really had accomplished something!"

Sister Taylor had a fun way of saying things. Once, she and her companion stayed a little late teaching a family and missed their last bus. They had to call the mission president in Honolulu, Jay Jenson, for help. As a result they got a rather stern reprimand for not using better judgment. Afterward Sister Taylor said, "I felt like a penny waiting for change." On another occasion, when she got sick, she described herself as feeling "like my parachute hadn't opened."

She was a go-getter, too. Once, when she arrived at the tabernacle in Honolulu and found the gate locked, she decided to climb the fence—in spite of the fact that she was wearing a dress. A brother from inside came out and told her to stop. That night she wrote in her journal, "Was my face red!"

Sister Taylor was a hard worker, but one morning when she was particularly tired she wrote: "Arose at 6:10. Took ten minutes to talk myself into the idea that it might be a good idea to get up." And yet when she had completed her first three months she wrote: "Today is my anniversary. Whee! Three months ago

I stepped off the boat to a new land and new people. I have loved every minute of it."

Sister Taylor was a tiny young woman who weighed 105 pounds at the beginning of her mission. She worried constantly about gaining weight. The Hawaiian and Japanese people were simply too good about feeding her. But she loved her experiences with these good people, and she talked constantly about her hopes for them.

And then one Sunday morning, bombs began to fall on Pearl Harbor. It was just a few miles from Kaliki, where she was living. She and her companion, along with other members at church that morning, assumed that a mock battle was taking place. When they finally learned that Japan had attacked, they were stunned. At that point it was hard to know what the results would be. "It was exciting," Sister Taylor wrote. "Wow—sent chills up and down our spines, fast!"

But the seriousness of the situation soon set in. Suddenly America was at war with Japan, and an entire mission in Hawaii was devoted to teaching Japanese Americans. On the mainland, a wave of hatred for Japanese people led to ugly incidents. And the government, fearing spies, eventually rounded up thousands of Japanese Americans and placed them in camps.

So how did Sister Taylor and the other missionaries handle this difficult situation? They simply returned to their work. Their love for the Japanese people didn't change. A nation had attacked America, but what did that have to do with the wonderful people in Hawaii who were of Japanese descent? Before the week was out, they were making visits and giving lessons again.

When Sister Taylor heard a rumor that the missionaries might be sent home, she said, "My heart fell to my feet!" But when she learned that it wasn't true, that they were actually staying, she wrote, "I could have jumped up and down with joy." And when she found out she was staying in Kaliki, she actually did jump: "Whee! I stay in Kaliki. Isn't that swelleree! . . . Sister Matthews and I took a flying leap in the air to meet each other and fell upside down."

At the time Pearl Harbor had been attacked, Sisters Taylor and Matthews were teaching a woman name Tanigawa. Sister Tanigawa always had a gift for them: a sack of oranges, a pineapple, a can of peaches. On one occasion she gave the sisters her last dollar. She had provided for her own needs, she said, and now she wanted to help the missionaries. She always thanked the sisters for the joy they brought her, and the sisters loved her for her grace, her kindness, and her love. Sister Taylor wrote, "I think how much she has helped me—in comparison to the little I may have done for her."

Sister Taylor and Sister Matthews volunteered to work with the Red Cross. They began to teach first-aid classes. But at the same time, they continued to teach Sister Tanigawa. On their first visit after the attack on Pearl Harbor, they discussed the war that had now been declared and the subject "Why doesn't God stop all this?" At the end of the discussion, Sister Tanigawa said, "Well, I guess all I need now is to be baptized." But she didn't really understand the need for baptism, and so the sisters agreed to discuss that subject the next time they came.

Sister Elizabeth Taylor

Eventually, for reasons of safety, the missionaries were transferred from the islands. Sister Taylor served the last six months of her mission in California. But until the day the missionaries shipped out, they continued their work with the Japanese people. And because they did, many souls were brought to the gospel. One of these conversions would later prove to be particularly important to the Church.

Before the attack on Pearl Harbor, a Japanese teenager began attending church and playing basketball with a team coached by some of the elders in the mission. Sister Taylor and other missionaries continued to work with the young man after the war broke out. They gave him lessons for some time before his family allowed him to be baptized.

If the missionaries had hardened their hearts against all Japanese, as so many Americans did, the boy never would have entered the Church. And a very great opportunity would have been lost. The young man was named Adney Komatsu. He would eventually become the first man of Asian descent to serve as a General Authority in the Church.

This chapter is based on Elizabeth Taylor Ottley, "Missionary Journals, 1941–1942," Archives of The Church of Jesus Christ of Latter-day Saints, Salt Lake City.

16

WARTIME MISSIONARY

During the Second World War, most young men in the Church were being drafted into military service, and few were left to serve missions. Thus Phileon B. Robinson of Boise, Idaho, was surprised to receive a mission call from his bishop in 1943. He had five children. Two of them were married, but one daughter's husband was in Europe "at the head of the battle," and the daughter and her baby were living with the Robinsons. Another daughter was attending Brigham Young University, and Phil, Jr., was getting ready to leave for the war himself. Added to this, Brother Robinson's wife, Dorothy, had been suffering with health problems.

Brother Robinson accepted the call, but a number of friends told him: "Phil, I wouldn't go. The Church can get along without you. Stay home where you belong and take care of your family."

Brother Robinson wondered. He asked the stake patriarch and another friend to come to his home and pray with him. After their prayers, M. J. Benson, the patriarch, said, "Phil, you go on your mission, just as you have promised to do, and when you return after two years, all will be well with your family."

And so Phil Robinson kept his word. He and his son left on the same train, one to fight a war, the other to teach peace. But Elder Robinson must have had his doubts for a time. His wife was so sick that she could hardly take care of herself. And Phil was sent to the mountain country of New Mexico, where the altitude didn't agree with him. He was sick for weeks before he was finally transferred to southern California.

Because of the shortage of missionaries, Elder Robinson was asked to labor alone for a time in the city of Oxnard. News from home was that Dorothy was still not well, and the family was pressed for money. Meanwhile, he found that few wanted to listen to his message. When he tried to teach the principles of the gospel, many asked him, "Why don't you go home to your family, or go to work and help win the war?"

Elder Robinson became so discouraged that he thought of taking a job. He could work eight hours a day and provide for his family, and he could do missionary work in the evenings and on his days off. It seemed a reasonable solution to his problems, and yet he knew it wasn't what he was called to do. And so he turned to the Lord. He prayed longer and harder than usual. When he got into bed, he felt a powerful presence in the room which spread through his body. A deep understanding came to him regarding the truth of the gospel principles— and how simple they were to explain. It was the most glorious and peaceful feeling he had ever experienced, and it changed his mission and his life.

Elder Robinson's work went much better after that experience, and he had many fine experiences. He felt very blessed, at one point in his mission, to be given a somewhat damaged tent that he could live in—with some donated furniture. This provided adequate housing and saved him money.

In 1944 Elder Robinson was transferred to the desert country not far from Death Valley. While laboring in Tehachapi, he was asked by his mission president to move on to Inyokern as soon as he could find a suitable place to live there. And so one rainy day he hitchhiked to Inyokern. He had no success in his search for a room, so he traveled on to Ridgecrest, about ten miles away. Here, too, he found nothing.

Elder Robinson had spent a long day sloshing through the rain, and he wondered why he had felt inspired that morning to make the trip. But he was walking down a road when a car pulled up. The driver, a woman he didn't know, asked him whether he needed a ride, as people often did in those days. Elder Robinson was happy for the ride. When Elder Robinson told the woman that he was an elder of the Church, she replied: "You are? Isn't that wonderful?"

Elder Robinson laughed and said, "I don't see anything wonderful about walking in all this rain and mud."

But the woman explained what she had meant. She said that her neighbor was a Latter-day Saint woman, and was very sick. That morning she had said that she wished she knew where she could find some Mormon elders. The woman driving the car thought it an odd coincidence that she would decide to drive to

Ridgecrest to see a friend, find the friend not home, and then spot Elder Robinson walking down the road. Elder Robinson, of course, took the opportunity to explain the power of healing and other principles of the gospel.

The woman took Elder Robinson to the home of the member, a Sister Maughan. There, Elder Robinson knocked on the door and then called out, "The Lord has sent me here to give you a blessing." Sister Maughan was joyous to let him in. She was pregnant and was in danger of miscarrying. She had been pregnant three times previously and had lost all three babies.

Elder Robinson blessed her, promising her she would carry the baby to full term and that the baby would be strong and healthy. He kept track of her in the coming months and learned that the promise was fulfilled. But even that night, as he found his way home, he already knew that the Lord had led him to Sister Maughan and would keep His promises to her.

Elder Robinson completed a successful mission and saw a number of people enter the Church. And his many faith-promoting experiences convinced him that he had done the right thing. When he returned home, another promise had been fulfilled. His family was doing better than ever. His wife's health had been restored, and all his children were prospering. Years later he would record that his children were all married in the temple and were well educated, and his grandchildren were now filling missions of their own. One of his sons served as a mission president. His example in serving a mission, when it was anything but convenient to do so, had established a family pattern that would continue in coming generations.

This chapter is based on Phileon B. Robinson, "Autobiography," MSS SC 524, Special Collections, Brigham Young University Library.

17

"HE SHALL TEACH YOU ALL THINGS"

In the spring of 1949, M. Russell Ballard, at that time a young missionary in England, was called as president of the Nottingham District. Elder Ballard had been on his mission less than a year, but already he was serving as the leader of thirty-four full-time missionaries.

The work was hard, and the missionaries were constantly searching for new ways to preach the gospel. Like many missionaries, the new district president wanted to do something dramatic. But when the opportunity came, it turned out to be a little more than he had bargained for.

The Midland Debating Society was an old and respected organization in England. A member of the society contacted Elder Ballard and asked whether an authority from the LDS church could make a presentation. Elder Ballard was sure that his mission president, Selvoy J. Boyer, would jump at the chance to present the message of the restored gospel to such a large and important group of people. The plan was for President Boyer to speak for forty-five minutes on the doctrines of the Church. Following his speech, those who wished to disagree would be allowed five minutes each. Then a question-and-answer period would follow.

Elder Ballard agreed to the format, set a date, and called the mission president. With great excitement he explained the opportunity. No Mormon missionary had spoken to this society since John A. Widtsoe—a powerful, even legendary missionary—had addressed the group twenty-five years before. Elder Ballard knew that President Boyer was a gospel scholar and a fine speaker. He would make a wonderful impression on the audience.

President Boyer listened to all this and then simply said, "Good luck, my boy."

Elder Ballard was taken back for a moment. The mission president had obviously misunderstood. So Elder Ballard started over. Once again he explained the arrangements, and this time he was very clear that it was the president who was to do the speaking.

President Boyer listened again, and this time he said, "The Lord bless you, my boy." Then he hung up the phone.

President Boyer, of course, recognized the importance of this experience to his young district president, but Elder Ballard wasn't looking that far ahead. More than anything else, Elder Ballard was scared. He didn't want to make a fool of himself. The audience would be full of older, experienced British debaters. He was a twenty-year-old American. Who would even take him seriously?

But Elder Ballard couldn't turn his back on the agreement with the debating society, nor on his mission president's charge to take the responsibility. And so he began to get ready. It was too late to do very much new preparation, but he certainly could fast and pray, and he asked his missionaries to do the same. He knew he would need the Lord's Spirit more than he ever had before.

On the day of the presentation, he asked all thirty-four missionaries in the district to come to the great hall in Nottingham where he would speak. When they arrived, he asked them to scatter themselves through the audience. The fact was, Elder Ballard was not even sure that he and the other missionaries were safe. A debate of this kind could create great emotion.

Over twelve hundred people came to hear what the Mormon missionary would have to say for himself. Elder Ballard stood before them, feeling very much alone. He gave a presentation that was simple yet profound. He explained that Christ had established a church during his time on earth, but that after Christ died, the church changed and the priesthood power disappeared. He explained how the doctrines had become confused after Christ's death, and he told about the Nicene Council, where early Christians had met and agreed to teachings that were not inspired. He then quoted scriptures showing that Christ had known this would happen. Finally, he explained how the true teachings of the gospel of Jesus Christ had been restored through the Prophet Joseph Smith.

When Elder Ballard was finished, members of the debating society—mature, educated men and women—rose one after another to disagree with him. They accused Mormons of false teachings. They attacked the Book of Mormon. They challenged the very idea that a restoration had been necessary. Elder Ballard listened and waited for his chance to defend the truth.

When the time was opened up for questions, Elder Ballard was nervous but eager to set the record straight. He had less than an hour to leave a lasting final impression on his listeners. But as the questions began, the missionary's anxiety turned into joy as he was filled with the power of the Holy Ghost.

Elder Ballard understood each question before it was finished, and the answer came to him immediately. He felt the Lord's Spirit, like a flood, filling him and guiding his responses. Sometimes he would actually quote scriptures by heart—verses he had read once or twice but certainly had never memorized. He spoke with clarity and yet with warmth and good will, and the audience was moved.

Time and again the questioners were impressed by Elder Ballard's answers as they heard his sound reasoning and felt the spirit with which he spoke. When the meeting finally ended, the crowd stood and gave him a standing ovation! Members of the debating society conversed with the many missionaries and congratulated Elder Ballard for his brilliant presentation.

But Elder Ballard knew better. Brilliance had nothing to do with it. He remembered the promise that the Savior had given to his apostles as he was preparing them for the time when he would no longer be with them. He told them that they would be able to teach the gospel because the Holy Ghost would guide them: "The comforter, which is the Holy Ghost, whom the Father will send in my name, he shall teach you all things, and bring all things to your remembrance, whatsoever I have said unto you." (John 14:26.)

Elder Ballard had felt alone as he had faced the great crowd, but he had not been alone. The Holy Ghost had been with him, ready to help him, and Elder Ballard's study of the gospel had prepared him. He had planted truths in his mind through his scripture study, and when he had needed those truths, the Holy Ghost had brought them to his remembrance—according to the promise.

That Sunday afternoon Elder Ballard had his first real experience with the power of the Holy Ghost, and he learned that he had nothing to fear when he was defending the gospel. Later in his mission he became a counselor to President Boyer, and then he extended his mission an extra five months to serve as counselor to President Boyer's replacement, Stayner Richards.

After his mission, he served in many callings in the Church. Eventually he was called to serve in the Quorum of the Twelve Apostles, just as his grandfather Melvin J. Ballard had done.

Throughout his ministry as a Church leader, he has trusted in the experience his mission president offered him—however much he feared it at the time. When speaking at press conferences or representing the Church in televised interviews, or in any other setting, he has taken comfort that the Lord would give him the answers he would need. Time and again he has seen how the Lord has fulfilled his promise "that the fulness of my gospel might be proclaimed by the weak and the simple unto the ends of the world, and before kings and rulers." (D&C 1:23.)

Elder Ballard has never forgotten the lessons he learned that day in England. Nor has he forgotten the lessons he *taught*. The importance of understanding the Apostasy and the Restoration has been a central theme in his ministry as an apostle of the Lord.

This chapter is based on interviews with Elder M. Russell Ballard by Dean Hughes and Tom Hughes, July 1995.

18

FIRST PRAYER

In 1963, Mary Ellen Edmunds and Carol Smithen became the first missionaries to work in Quezon City in the Philippines. Later the city would become the headquarters of an entire mission, but at the time it was part of the Philippines Zone of the Southern Far East Mission. Eventually Sister Smithen received a new companion, and Mary Jane Davidson was assigned to work with Sister Edmunds.

Early the next year, Sister Edmunds and Sister Davidson were going door to door "tracting," and they were not doing very well. They really weren't in the mood to work that morning, and they knew what that meant: they didn't have the Spirit. So they stopped on the street, each said a silent prayer, and then they approached the next house. When they rang the doorbell, an eye soon appeared in a little peephole. The sisters told the man on the other side of the peephole that they were missionaries and would like to visit with him for a few minutes.

"I am Cat-o-leek," the man said. At that time, the missionaries did not learn the Filipino languages as they do now. Most people did speak at least some English, but the sisters could tell that this man did not speak a great deal. They both felt strongly prompted, however, to keep trying, and finally he agreed to let them come in.

The man told the sisters that his name was Felixberto S. Ocampo. He was a somewhat older man with an impressive appearance and dark, graying hair. That hair, along with his kindly manner, reminded the sisters of President David O. McKay.

As the sisters sat down to talk with Mr. Ocampo, the Spirit was telling both of them not to present a lesson but to tell him about Joseph Smith's first vision. And so Sister Edmunds told the story, using simple English words so that he

64

could understand. As she spoke, however, she was struck by the way he listened with full attention and great interest.

When Sister Edmunds finished the story, Mr. Ocampo's response was unlike any she had experienced before. "That is a beautiful story," he said. "Can you tell me again?"

This time Sister Davidson gave the account, and again the missionaries were moved by the great concentration and the conviction in Mr. Ocampo's eyes. This time his reply was even more surprising: "This is a very beautiful story. Can you tell me one more time?"

The missionaries had to take turns this time. They were so moved by the spirit of this good man, the obvious joy he was receiving in hearing about Joseph Smith, that neither could talk very long without crying. When they made it through the story the third time, Mr. Ocampo asked, "Where is he now?"

The sisters told him that Joseph Smith was dead, and they were amazed to see

Sister Mary Jane Davidson (left) and Sister Mary Ellen Edmunds

how saddened Mr. Ocampo appeared. He had just heard the wonderful news that God had spoken to a man on earth, and now he was disappointed and sorrowful to learn that this prophet was already gone. He then asked, "How did he die?" The sisters were deeply hurt to have to tell him that Joseph Smith had been murdered.

"*Why?* Why did they do this?" Mr. Ocampo asked, with pain in his voice and in his eyes.

All their lives the sisters had heard the story, they knew of Joseph Smith's life and death, but this man was making it all new for them. He believed their account—the Spirit had told him it was true—and now he was pained at the loss of this prophet he had never known, disturbed to think that God would call a prophet and people would then take his life.

"If I have been alive," Mr. Ocampo said, in his halting English, "I will protect his life with my life."

Sister Edmunds and Sister Davidson reassured Mr. Ocampo that a prophet was, in fact, still upon the earth, and they promised to return and continue to teach him. When they arrived for their second visit, Mr. Ocampo told them, "Oh, Sisters, I have a beautiful story to tell you." What he told them was the account he had read in a pamphlet that they had given him during their first visit. It was the story of Joseph's Smith's vision along with other events in his life. He rehearsed the story in such detail that they could tell he had read it many times. They had read the pamphlet, of course, and they knew all about the Prophet Joseph, but when they heard him give his version, charged with his belief and his excitement, they seemed to hear it for the first time.

During one visit, the sisters asked Mr. Ocampo whether he prayed. "Oh, yes, sisters," he said (pronouncing the word "seesters"). "I pray every day." So they taught him the principles of prayer and, from that time on, asked him to pray at the beginning or end of their meetings. He asked each time if it would be all right if he prayed in Tagalog, his own language. They said that was fine. They didn't understand much of what he said in these prayers, but they felt his good spirit.

Mr. Ocampo received all the missionary lessons with the same spirit, and he accepted baptism. One Sunday soon after he was baptized, the branch president asked him to pray in Church, but Brother Ocampo said he couldn't. The sisters were surprised. When they visited him the next time, he explained. "I want to pray the way *you* pray," he said, and it was only then that they discovered he had been saying memorized prayers, not speaking to the Lord in his own words.

The sisters repeated for him the elements of a prayer, and this time he understood. The idea that he could actually talk with his Heavenly Father was wonderful to him. "I'll be the one to pray this time," he told the sisters. "I'll use English. If I say something wrong, you can tell me."

They knelt together, and then he paused for a very long time as he considered what he wanted to say. This was no ordinary event, the sisters realized; this man of faith was about to converse with the Lord for the first time. He wanted to choose the right words. Both sisters were weeping before Brother Ocampo even began to pray.

He worked hard for the right English words as he began, but the sisters felt no need to correct anything he said. Now and again he would stop and say, "Sisters, this is very beautiful, no?"

They would nod, tears streaming down their faces. This was clearly the most beautiful prayer either had ever heard.

"If I am slow, will He wait for me?" he asked at one point.

"Yes," the sisters told him. "Take all the time you want."

And finally he asked, "Sisters, does Heavenly Father know Tagalog?"

They assured him that the Lord knew every language, and in response Brother Ocampo asked whether he could finish in his own language. They said he could, and then they heard him pour out his feelings fluently, in his native tongue, and they understood the spirit of what he said.

Brother Ocampo was a steadfast member of the Church until he died. His faith was a power to all who knew him. And Sister Edmunds and Sister Davidson were better people for having met him. They had learned of their prophet as though for the first time. They had also heard a man speak with God with such pleasure and intimacy that their own prayers would be changed forever.

This chapter is based on interviews with Mary Ellen Edmunds by Dean Hughes, May 1995.

19

AFRICA: THE LONG WAIT ENDS

T he gospel reached Africa in a peculiar way. In other parts of the world, the Church usually sends missionaries to seek out those who are willing to listen and accept the message of the Restoration. In Africa, the people begged the Church to come. In Nigeria and Ghana there were groups of people who knew the message, had already accepted it, and wanted Church leaders to bring missionaries who could baptize them and establish branches.

Africans had learned about the Church in various ways. Most often it was through Church pamphlets that had found their way to those who read and believed them. Eventually many people, often not knowing that others shared their convictions, had come to believe in Joseph Smith as a prophet. Some of these people received visions or miraculous experiences that prepared them to accept the Church before they actually learned of it.

In 1960, Church leaders asked Glen G. Fisher, a mission president returning from the South African Mission, to stop in Lagos, the capital of Nigeria. They wanted him to meet with a group of Nigerians who had discovered the Church and desired to be taught. President Fisher was able to locate three of the leaders of this group, and when he introduced himself as a Mormon missionary, he was received with great joy. The men, each in turn, grabbed his hand in both of theirs, their faces lighting up with enthusiasm. Then they sat with President Fisher and for three hours asked him questions about the teachings of the Church.

Using just a few missionary pamphlets, these Nigerians had taught their friends, and the word had spread. They had established two large groups, totaling more than a thousand people, who met together to learn the principles of the gospel. Not a single one of them smoked or drank alcohol. Even though they were all very poor, they paid tithing on their small incomes, and with that money had built two little chapels.

However, great obstacles had to be overcome before missionaries could be sent to Africa. It was a vast continent, constantly torn by civil wars. Some countries opposed foreign missionaries and wouldn't grant travel visas. Transportation and communication between branches would be difficult. The Church could not establish branches in a place where no experienced leadership existed.

Church leaders knew that to send missionaries to Africa was to take on a huge, complex job, and they didn't feel prepared to do that—yet. But they did know that the gospel would be preached in all the world, and the day of Africa was not far off. The Lord was preparing the people. More and more contacts were coming from Africans who were trying to set up the Church on their own.

Not until 1978 was an official mission opened in Nigeria. Even after Church leaders had committed to begin the work, visa problems and government red tape further delayed the process. But in August 1978, Edwin Cannon and Merrill Bateman were sent to check on the groups in Nigeria and Ghana and to bring back a recommendation about what steps should be taken to establish authorized branches of the Church. These men returned with the advice that it was time to move ahead.

Moving quickly, Church leaders assigned Elder Cannon and his wife, Janath, along with Elder Rendell Mabey and his wife, Rachel, to take the long-awaited ordinances to the people of west Africa. Upon arriving, they taught the people in groups, baptized them, and organized branches of the Church on the foundation established by the people themselves.

For those who had waited so long for priesthood authority, and for leaders from the Church, the joy was unspeakable. Most of the stories of those who were finally baptized—and how they first learned of the gospel—are remarkable. The account of the first black couple to become members of the Church in Nigeria is just one example of the kind of people the Cannons and Mabeys met there.

Anthony Uzodimma Obinna and his wife, Fidelia Njoku Obinna, had married in 1950. Fidelia was an orphan who, when younger, had supported her younger brothers and sisters. She had never had the opportunity to receive an education. Her husband, however, had gone to school and had become a teacher. Life for this couple was not easy, but they worked hard and were good and honest. Then, a series of dreams or visions changed their lives.

Starting in 1965, Anthony Obinna was visited in a dream by a tall man carrying a walking stick. He appeared on three different occasions, but in one of the dreams he took Brother Obinna to a beautiful building and showed him through it. During the Nigerian civil war that took place at that time, Brother Obinna was confined to his house. One day he picked up an old copy of the *Reader's Digest:*

> I opened it to page 34 and saw a picture of the same beautiful building I had been shown around in my dream, and immediately I recognized it. The heading was "The March of the Mormons." I had never before heard the word *Mormons.* I started to read the story because of the picture of the building I had seen in my dream. I discovered that it was all about The Church of Jesus Christ of Latter-day Saints.
>
> From the time I finished reading the story, I had no rest of mind any longer. My whole attention was focused on my new discovery. I rushed out immediately to tell my brothers, who were all amazed and astonished to hear the story.

Brother Obinna waited six years for the war to end so he could get a letter to Salt Lake City. He received books and pamphlets, but he was told that the Church could not yet come to Nigeria. The Obinnas had grown used to waiting. They continued to study the gospel and to pray that the Church would be brought to them soon.

Seven more years passed. The waiting ended on November 21, 1978, when the Obinnas were baptized. Brother Obinna was set apart as branch president over the Aboh Mbaise Branch, with his two brothers, Francis and Raymond, called as his counselors. Sister Obinna became the first Relief Society president in the new branch.

The Obinnas, like so many other Africans, were their own missionaries for thirteen years. They had read and prayed and grown closer to the Lord through all the waiting. And all across the continent, especially in west Africa, others were having similar experiences. The Cannons and Mabeys baptized thousands of people and organized many branches. But the work was only beginning. The day of Africa had finally arrived.

For further reading, see Alexander B. Morrison, *The Dawning of a Brighter Day: The Church in Black Africa* (Salt Lake City: Deseret Book Co., 1990).

70

20

AMAZING GROWTH IN MEXICO CITY

Since the beginning of the Restoration, thousands of missionaries have worked with extraordinary commitment. In the early years they were often turned away, insulted, or even physically attacked. But the missionaries never lost faith in their message. They baptized those who believed and continued to plant seeds wherever they could. In the second half of the twentieth century, the harvest began to increase dramatically, with many thousands of new converts coming into the Church.

For many years, hundreds of missionaries had labored in Mexico and in Central and South America with only limited success. But in the 1960s, people in Spanish-speaking countries began to join the Church in astounding numbers. By the middle of the 1970s, in the Mexico City area, thousands of converts were joining the Church every year. This tremendous surge of growth was exciting but challenging. Many leaders had to be found among these converts, and often they were called to lead shortly after they joined the Church.

In 1975, Elder Howard W. Hunter of the Council of the Twelve consulted with other Church leaders and concluded that the stakes in the Mexico City area needed to be realigned to deal with all this growth. It was important to decrease the geographical size of the stakes in order to reduce travel. And the number of stakes would have to be increased in order to handle all the new converts. The conclusion Elder Hunter reached was to expand five stakes into *fifteen*. After he received approval from President Spencer W. Kimball and the First Presidency, the time to make the change was set. It would all happen on one weekend!

Elder Hunter and his wife, Claire, flew to Mexico City on Thursday, November 6, 1975. Joining Elder Hunter were Elder J. Thomas Fyans, an Assistant to the Quorum of the Twelve, four Regional Representatives, and mission president Lester B. Whetten. On Friday morning Elder Hunter and Elder

Fyans began to interview potential stake presidents. It took them twelve hours to interview two hundred men, but at the end of the day they had chosen and called the fifteen stake presidents.

The new stake presidents had to select their counselors quickly, and then these presidencies had to begin choosing their high councils and bishops. Following that, the new bishops had to choose counselors and begin to organize realigned wards. What was required was a lot of prayer and inspiration—with no time to spare.

The plan had been to hold one huge meeting in the National Auditorium, which could hold eighteen thousand people. In that setting the stakes could be divided and all the new stake presidencies could then be sustained. But at the last minute, officials who operated the National Auditorium cancelled the Church's reservation and replaced the Church meeting with a rock concert.

Left with no other building that would hold so many members, Elder Hunter decided to hold six separate stake conference meetings in two days: three on Saturday and three on Sunday. Starting on Saturday morning, Elder Hunter and Elder Fyans attended eighteen hours of conference meetings, traveled nine hours, ate when they could—and got a *little* sleep.

On Saturday morning, Elder Hunter officiated as one stake was split into two and the members sustained the new stake presidencies. In the middle of the day he divided another stake into three, and later in the afternoon he split one more stake into two. In between meetings and travel, all the new leaders had to be set apart, and many of them were ordained as high priests.

The work ended at about midnight—except that the day wasn't really finished. Elder Hunter told a *Church News* reporter:

> It was late when we got home, and we were tired after three conferences, the organization of seven stakes, and all the ordaining and setting apart. Sister Fyans prepared a lunch for us, and Brother Fyans and Claire and I left for Cuautla a little after midnight so we could be there for an early-morning conference.
>
> The trip at night takes only two hours, while in the morning it would take much longer. By 2:30 A.M. we were in bed at the Hotel Visca.

Conference began at seven the next morning. Elder Hunter split the stake and sustained two new stake presidencies, two new high councils, and many bish-oprics. As the General Authorities left that conference, the members, according to Elder Hunter, "sang to us, with tears in their eyes, the song of love and affec-tion, 'La Golondrina.'"

And then the next dash began—back into the city. But traffic was bad, even on Sunday, and Elder Hunter and Elder Fyans were late arriving for the mid-day session. That didn't help, because this was the biggest job yet: one stake was being split into four.

The last stake was finally divided late that day, and around midnight, once again, the job was done. In one weekend, 45 men in 15 stake presidencies had been called and set apart; approximately 150 new high councilors had been placed in office (about 30 more would have to be called later). In 96 wards, 288 bishopric members had also been called.

Ten of the fifteen new stake presidents were under forty years of age. Three were still in their twenties. One of them was twenty-four! In most cases, these were not experienced leaders with a lifetime of training in the Church. They were young men, mostly converts. They were going to have to grow quickly, handle great challenges, and deal with the ongoing growth they would be see-ing. But Elder Hunter had no doubt they would meet the challenge with com-mitment and inspiration.

Elder Hunter, in his typically humble way, summed up the weekend: "After completing the work, we got home about midnight, exhausted but with a feel-ing of accomplishment." In his diary he wrote, "I doubt there has ever been such a mass organization in the Church." He needn't have wondered. Nothing even close to this had happened before.

Elder Hunter and Elder Fyans stayed in Mexico the next week. They held a three-day seminar for mission presidents and organized another stake in Vera Cruz. And then, on the way home, Elder Hunter made a stop in Houston. This was an easy job: he only had to split one stake into two. But on one trip he had actually created or reorganized eighteen stakes of the Church.

For years afterward, other General Authorities and even President Kimball teased Elder Hunter about his famous reorganization trip to Mexico City. In 1976, when Elder Hunter returned from another trip to Mexico, President

Kimball asked him why he had managed to create only three new stakes. And when Elder Bruce R. McConkie organized five stakes in South America on one trip, President Kimball joked that he was going after Elder Hunter's record.

Growth in Mexico would continue at a rapid pace, however, and Elder Hunter's wisdom would become clear. Within the next few years, more stakes would be created throughout the nation, and the fifteen stakes in Mexico City, established and ready to deal with the many new members, "filled up" quickly. In fact, expansion of membership in all Latin American countries has continued at a rate that has made Spanish easily the second most common language of the Church. Some predict that if membership growth continues at a similar pace, the day could come that more Latter-day Saints will speak Spanish than English.

Apostles are leaders, and they do much to guide all the affairs of the Church. But they are also missionaries. Their special calling is to serve as witnesses of Jesus Christ. When Elder Hunter traveled to Mexico to realign the stakes, he was conducting the business of the Church, but he was also ministering to the people and bringing the new converts into the fold. On that dramatic weekend and throughout his ministry, he fulfilled the Savior's instruction to His apostles of old: "Go ye therefore, and teach all nations." (Matthew 28:19.)

For further reading, see Eleanor Knowles, *Howard W. Hunter* (Salt Lake City: Deseret Book Co., 1994); and "Growth in Mexican Cities Explodes into Sixteen Stakes," *Church News,* 22 November 1975, pp. 3, 14–15.

21

"SEND ME FOOD OR I WILL DIE"

It would be interesting to know the percentage of missionaries who, after serving for a week or two, would give almost *anything* to come home. One missionary who was completely honest about her feelings, both in her journal and in her letters home, was a young woman from Salt Lake City named Ann Crebs. Sister Crebs served in Thailand in 1983 and 1984.

As Sister Crebs flew to Thailand, fresh from the Missionary Training Center, she was certain she would be an exceptional missionary. But the moment she stepped off that airplane, optimism turned to worry. A blast of overwhelmingly humid heat hit her. The smells outside were nauseating, and nothing seemed familiar. In those first weeks she wrote home: "I am on the verge of crying at all times. It's hard to see a light ahead. I can't understand one thing that is said to me. . . . *Please* put my name in at the temple and pray for me."

Over the next few weeks, she sent home letters that described all the things she hated about Thailand:

> I am *constantly* thirsty. The kitchen is outside of the house. I *hate* to go in there. It is moldy and full of various bugs. We have a huge "dug gaa" thing that looks like a mini crocodile that goes in there every evening and makes really loud noises. This place reminds me of the scriptures where it talks about "every creeping and crawling thing that walked on the earth," or however it goes.
>
> We have to take "dipper" showers. We just dip out water from a barrel and pour it down our bodies. OOOHHH. No matter how hot it gets, I can't quite get used to that cold water running down my back.
>
> I went to the branch for the first time yesterday. I was totally blown away. I didn't understand one thing that was said. There were about 20 people there including missionaries. They meet in a house. . . . I *could NOT* believe that missionaries have been coming to Chiang Mai for *years* and only 20 people at church to show for it.

You have never seen conditions like the ones in Thailand. . . . Some Thais have little stands on the streets and then live above them, but there are millions who just live in little shacks. They sit around or sleep all day in the dirt. Most of the shacks have one whole open side and lots of bugs!

They have the grossest things to eat, and the smells are SO FOUL! PLEASE!!! SEND ME FOOD OR I WILL *DIE* OUT HERE.

There are bugs EVERYWHERE. I had to stop wearing lip gloss because the bugs stick to my lips.

Now besides my constant headaches I have a heat rash. It's like you get used to the fact that you will never feel tip top here. . . . My hair is a total BOOF—it is so humid. You might as well use me for a lamp shade.

I hope this letter hasn't been too negative, but I haven't had any positive experiences yet.

I have NEVER been *SO LONELY*. I am all alone.

Needless to say, if Sister Crebs could have found an easy way out, she would have headed home. But she had committed to serve, and she didn't want to give up. Gradually, she became able to contribute and not just tag along. The "impossible" language became something less of a mystery. Thailand, by law, would not allow door-to-door contacting, so Sister Crebs and her companion began to try new proselyting ideas. For one thing, they did good deeds for people. Not only did they create a good impression in the community, but doors were opened to them.

"I am getting caught up in the work now and am actually enjoying it a bit," she admitted. She found scriptures that helped her, and she prayed constantly for strength. She also began to change her feelings about the Thai people:

We were riding our bikes out in a total rainstorm and had 15 miles to go. It was like a rain blizzard, and we were SOAKED. Some girls motioned to us and had us stand under their porch for a while—they were so concerned about us. Then a man stopped on his motorcycle and gave me his rain poncho. We offered to pay him or to return it later, but he said no. Then he disappeared into the distance. I am really growing to love these people!

I can't believe I am saying this, but I LOVE OUR BRANCH! . . . When I first came I was appalled, but now I can see that we are actually lucky. We've got some good members, very few, but they keep things above water.

My new companion (a Thai) has sacrificed so much to be here. . . . They don't have a separation of state and religion in Thailand, so when people convert, you are not only asking them to change religions but also to give up so many of their traditions and holidays. It is too overwhelmingly embarrassing to their parents, and they must disown their children who convert in order to save face. So my companion, like so many members, has come out here to serve for 18 months with NO love and no support.

One day Sister Crebs and her companion went to visit a young woman named Tawn Tip. They had been teaching her the missionary lessons. They found, however, that she was very sick and in intensive care in a hospital. The sisters found two elders and brought them back to give her a blessing. Two days later Tawn Tip was back on her feet and home. With tears in her eyes she greeted the sisters, her heart full of joy and appreciation. Sister Crebs could hardly believe that the young woman was grasping *her* and thanking *her*: "By then we were all crying, and my heart was full of love for her and the fact that I had played a small part in such a miracle. It was at that moment I realized I do have something to offer. I can be an instrument even if I can't understand and am struggling."

Sister Crebs had already controlled her desire to run from the challenge, but now something inside herself was beginning to change. And once that happened, Thailand seemed to change before her eyes. She began to understand many things that had once seemed strange simply because they were different from what she had experienced in her own country:

> I want to take back all those things I said about the Thai people! Thai people are SO neat! . . . You can learn so much from them. In a lot of ways, they're better than Americans. They really are a hard-working people, too. Sometimes during the day you might see them sleeping, but that's because they start work at 4:00 or 5:00 in the morning to avoid the mid-day heat. . . . I really have been blessed with the ability to relate well to them and to hit if off with them. I have such a love for them, and they also seem to care for me.

By the time Sister Crebs finished her mission, she could walk into the kitchen and spot one of those big "crocodile-looking" things—a huge lizard—

77

and say, "He makes me nervous, but I just stay in my corner, and so far he has just stayed in his." One night she and her companion were sleeping on the floor at a zone conference when Sister Crebs felt something in her hair. She flipped the light on, and the floor seemed to move with cockroaches. She and her companion each grabbed a shoe, pounded away at them and then swept them outside. "No big deal," she told her parents in a letter.

On another occasion, she was teaching a young companion who was going through the agonies of adjustment herself. After standing for three days by a missionary display, the companion questioned whether there was any point in just waiting all day and getting so few results. But Sister Crebs had learned patience. On the fourth day, the sisters got three referrals. "And ONE WAS A FAMILY!!!" she exclaimed.

The months began to roll faster, and no longer were Sister Crebs's letters focused on the heat and the bugs and the mission that would last forever. Her talk was constantly of love for the people, baptisms, working with the good members, and all the satisfactions of being a missionary. As time was running out on her mission, she wrote home:

> I am being a missionary to its fullest, and I *LOVE* it. . . . I just don't know how I can leave here—really. I know a year and a half ago I was on the other side of the world saying the same thing! OH! I've come so far and learned so much since then. At home I was just another face in the crowd—here I feel I am making an important contribution. . . . I wake up each morning and I say, "Okay, today I am going to hang on to every minute," and the next thing I know, it has passed and it is gone from my reach forever. . . . A year and a half ago I would have DIED to be home hanging out and cruising around. Now all I can think about is how much I am needed here and all the work there is still to do.

Ann Crebs still reflects often on her experience as a missionary. One thing she learned about herself was that before her mission she had tended to quit things that were difficult. But she didn't quit her mission, and she is now a stronger, better person as a result. That discipline helps her as a wife, a mother, a Church leader—and in every facet of her life. But she also came home from Thailand with a changed heart—more open to love for people different from herself, more moved by the gospel of Jesus Christ.

Ann Crebs, now Ann Weight, thinks of her time in Thailand with great fondness. She hasn't forgotten how hard the work was, but she is thankful she served, and even more thankful for what Thailand did for her. And, by the way, she often cooks Thai dishes. She loves the food!

This chapter is based on interviews with Ann Crebs Weight by Dean Hughes, February 1995; and unpublished letters and diaries in possession of Ann Crebs Weight.

22

NATIVE MISSIONARIES IN CHILE

Elder W. Craig Zwick served as president of the Chile Santiago South Mission from 1989 to 1992. He presided over a mission that saw more than five thousand convert baptisms per year. The growth was exciting as well as challenging for President Zwick and his wife, Jan. But one of the most satisfying experiences of their mission was to see young Chileans come into the mission field and not only experience success but also develop the leadership skills they needed to serve in their home wards and stakes.

In 1990, a young man named Edwin Varela arrived in the Santiago South Mission. He was twenty-three years old and had graduated in mathematics from a university in Antofagasta, where he had grown up. He had been raised in a humble home in this desert town in northern Chile. His father, part Peruvian and part Bolivian, worked in a large copper mine where most of the people in the area worked. Elder Varela had joined the Church with his parents and two brothers.

When President Zwick met Elder Varela, he was immediately impressed with his intelligence, his humility, and his obvious leadership ability. Within four months Elder Varela was already serving as a zone leader. At a conference shortly after receiving this assignment, Elder Varela stunned his fellow missionaries by telling them in a testimony meeting that the two missionaries who had taught and baptized him were still serving on their missions. In other words, Elder Varela had been a member of the Church only one year when he had entered the mission field.

Elder Varela became everything President Zwick expected. He served as a trainer for many missionaries, including several from North America. He spoke English quite well, and he was sensitive to the adjustment problems of the young missionaries who were coming to a new culture. After serving as a leader throughout his mission and having great success bringing many converts into the Church, Elder Varela was released just before the Zwicks completed their own term of service. About two weeks later Elder Varela returned to Santiago to be married in the temple. At the same time, he and his brothers were sealed to their parents.

Elder Varela and his new wife returned to his hometown, and only three months later he was called to serve in a bishopric. It will be he, and other young men and women like him, who will step forward to lead the thousands of converts constantly entering the waters of baptism throughout the nation.

During the time that the Zwicks served, about a fourth of the elders were native Chileans, but closer to half of the sisters were Chileans. The story of Sister Claudia Legues and Sister Francisca Ruiz offers an example of the way native missionaries in Chile are strengthening themselves and each other.

Sisters Legues and Ruiz were from Punta Arenas, on the southern tip of Chile, where penguins can be found and the Antarctic is not far away. They were both converts to the Church, and they worked in the same office in Punta Arenas. Sister Legues had become less active in the Church, and it was Sister Ruiz who prodded her to become more involved. Sister Legues not only got involved, but she got excited about going on a mission. Sister Ruiz had also thought about a mission but wasn't sure she was ready to serve.

Sister Legues received her mission call, entered the Chilean missionary training center, and then began her mission in the Santiago South Mission. Excited about the work, she began to write her friend, Sister Ruiz, encouraging her to accept a call. That was all the push Sister Ruiz needed. She, too, entered the Lord's service and was called to the same mission.

When Sister Ruiz sat down for the first time with President Zwick, she told him about her friend who was in the mission and who had played such a large role in her choosing to enter the mission field. President Zwick prayed to know who should be the trainer for Sister Ruiz. The answer was clear, and he felt it was right. He assigned Sister Legues to train Sister Ruiz as her first companion.

When the two friends first saw each other, they embraced and shed tears of love for the Savior and for each other. But then they got to work. Their hard work and obedient service throughout their missions provided a positive example to other missionaries.

The Zwicks also saw many examples of Chilean and North American missionaries working well together. One native missionary, Sister Mayela Muñoz, worked with Sister Rebecca Gudgell from Bountiful, Utah. While serving

together in Rengo, a town south of Santiago, they met a woman named Isabel Abarca. She had first been taught the gospel in 1975 by a young Chilean missionary named Gonzalo Sepulveda. Her sister and mother had joined the Church, but Isabel had remained a Catholic and had become a nun. She had never forgotten the principles she had been taught, however, and she observed what the Church did

Sister Rebecca Gudgell (left), Isabel Abarca, and Sister Mayela Muñoz outside an LDS meetinghouse on the day of Isabel's baptism

for her family over those seventeen years. And so she allowed herself to be taught again, this time by Sisters Muñoz and Gudgell, and she accepted the gospel. Needless to say, it was no easy choice for her, but she gave up her vows as a nun and joined the Church.

When it came time for her baptism, Isabel Abarca asked for Elder Sepulveda, the missionary who had taught her long before, to perform the ordinance. After his mission he had served long and well in many leadership positions, and he was now a Regional Representative of the Church. He was only too happy to baptize Sister Abarca and unite her again with her family. By this time her brother, too, had joined the Church.

Some of the Chilean missionaries had to sell musical instruments or other possessions to finance their missions. Many worked multiple jobs to raise sufficient funds for their missions, and many served in spite of parents who would not or could not support them. Most came from humble backgrounds. In many cases the missionaries who came from LDS families had never been sealed in the temple. But at the end of their missions, the families would often travel, at great sacrifice, to Santiago, where they could pick up their missionary and receive their endowments and sealings in the Santiago Chile Temple. These families would then return home, and the young returned missionaries would use the faith and understanding they had gained to strengthen the members in their wards and stakes.

The membership of the Church is growing very fast in Chile. Missionaries in Chilean missions spend only about 20 percent of their time finding people to teach. They spend the balance of their time teaching. This not only leads to many baptisms, but it also develops young people into fine teachers and leaders. As the growth continues, it will be these returned missionaries who will become the leaders in their wards and stakes and will provide the strong Melchizedek Priesthood base that is necessary to sustain the rapid expansion of the Church in that land.

In much the same way, President Zwick also grew through his missionary experience and returned home to lead. In 1995 he was called to serve as a General Authority in the First Quorum of the Seventy.

This chapter is based on interviews with Elder and Sister W. Craig Zwick by Dean Hughes, March 1995.

23

BEHIND THE IRON CURTAIN

At the end of World War II, Germany was occupied by the victorious armies. In eastern Germany, the Soviet Union established a communist government. Many citizens began to flee to western Germany. Fences had to be built to hold the people in, and finally, in 1961, an ugly cement-and-block wall was built through the center of Berlin. On the western side of the wall people retained their freedoms, but in the German Democratic Republic, usually known as East Germany, the government stopped free elections and controlled access to information.

In West Germany people recovered from the war, and in time the nation prospered. But in the east, the citizens got by with very little, and life was often dull and difficult. Along the walls and fences of East Germany was a barren strip of land, a "dead zone." Guards with guns and attack dogs watched these areas day and night to keep people from escaping. These dead zones, extending not only through Germany but along the borders of other communist countries, came to be known as the "iron curtain."

The communist government in East Germany was opposed to religion, but officials did not stop people from worshipping. The Latter-day Saints there, though not great in number, managed not only to survive but also to strengthen themselves.

Gradually, the East German government gained favorable impressions of their LDS citizens. Mormons were industrious people with good families. They also believed in "obeying, honoring, and sustaining the law." (Article of Faith12.) Because of this, the government gradually opened more opportunities to them.

In 1968, Elder Thomas S. Monson was allowed to visit and speak to members of the Church in East Germany. He felt inspired to tell them that if they kept God's commandments, the day would come when "every blessing any member of the Church enjoys in any other country" would be theirs. After that, he prayed and worked hard to negotiate with government leaders to make that prophecy come true. Approval came to build churches, but the Saints had no temple. They didn't have *all* the blessings other members enjoyed. When President Monson tried to obtain permission for the members to travel to Switzerland, a government official asked why the Church didn't build a temple in East Germany.

It was a stunning moment—and one no one could have expected. At least no one but President Monson. He had promised the Saints, and now he was seeing the Lord soften the hearts of communist officials. Details were worked out, and a temple was built in Freiberg. And then, in similar negotiations, President Monson asked for permission to establish a mission. Once again a door was opened that had seemed closed forever.

The Germany Dresden Mission opened when eight experienced elders, chosen from the five German-speaking missions then in Europe, crossed the border in Berlin on March 30, 1989. They were led by President Wolfgang Paul, who had been serving as president of the Germany Hamburg Mission. Two days later, at general conference in Salt Lake City, Church leaders announced the new mission. President Monson told the dramatic story of missionaries crossing the iron curtain—and how it had all come about.

It was a remarkable moment in history. A whole new era of missionary work had opened. And members throughout the world knew that the day was almost at hand when the gospel would be preached in *every* part of the world, as the scriptures promise.

Inside East Germany, the reception the missionaries received was overwhelming. President Paul took the missionaries to four cities: East Berlin, Dresden, Leipzig, and Zwickau. Among the last to be dropped off was Elder Chris Karpowitz. He and his companion were placed in Zwickau, in southern East Germany.

Most of the ward members were excitedly waiting for the missionaries when they arrived. These people had been cut off from direct contact with the Church for a whole generation. They had hardly dared to dream that missionaries would ever return to them. Many tears were shed as everyone took turns greeting the elders.

What was even more amazing was the welcome the missionaries received from the non-Mormon people. Americans were a novelty, fascinating to the local citizens. All the missionaries had to do was hold open houses, and people came in great numbers. East Germans were a people searching for answers, and they were eager to know what these Americans had to say.

In Dresden and Leipzig, many people had been attending church for years without having been baptized. The missionaries began baptizing them. Elder Karpowitz and his companion began to teach many friends of the Saints along with the many people they were meeting at their open houses. From the very beginning, finding people to teach was not a problem. The missionaries put in long, hard days and taught many discussions. They often split up, each taking a member along so they could double their capacity to teach.

All the while, these young men were being watched everywhere they went. They were followed by government officials and observed by the public at every step. They had to be very wise for such young men, diplomats in a still tense situation. But they had been chosen exactly because they were skilled, able missionaries, and they handled the challenge well.

After serving several months in Zwickau, Elder Karpowitz was transferred to the city of Halle. This was a university town, and by that time many students in the country were staging protests against communism. It was a frightening time, since the government was quick to use force against these protestors.

One night Elder Karpowitz and his companion were walking to an appointment when they came to a street that was strangely empty and silent. They felt a spirit they didn't like, so they avoided the street and took a back way to their appointment. The people the elders taught that night knew what was going on. Students were meeting at that very moment, discussing the next step in the revolt.

The next day, the elders learned that during the student meeting the protestors were attacked and beaten by the communist police, known as the Stazi. The quiet street the elders had avoided was suddenly turned into a scene of bloodshed and brutality. The missionaries knew the Lord had guided them away from a place of great danger.

The protests didn't end, and Elder Karpowitz was still in Halle on the day the Berlin Wall came down. He watched as the people lined up to get their passports stamped so they could have the joy of spending one day in the West—away from the oppression they had known so long.

And yet the day had its downside for the missionaries. The East German people had had very few of the material things most people in other countries took for granted. Living with so much hardship, they searched for answers and wondered about the meaning of life. Once they began to see the chance to have more and to live better, these same people were much less interested in religion. The work that had gone so fast began to slow, and the missionaries had to work hard, as missionaries usually do, just to get people to listen to them.

The first eight missionaries, however, knew they had served at an important moment in history. The gospel must be taught in all the world. And they had begun the work in eastern Europe, where hundreds of missionaries are now serving.

This chapter is based on interviews with Chris Karpowitz by Tom Hughes, March 1995.

24

THE CHAPMAN BROTHERS OF AUSTRALIA

In 1991, John Stohlton had just begun to serve as president of the Australia Melbourne Mission along with his wife, Colleen. During a conference, President Stohlton pointed to an elder he didn't yet know well and asked him to read a scripture. The missionary began to rise to his feet when his companion reached out and grabbed his shoulder, as though to hold him down. The elder shrugged off his companion's grasp and stood anyway. He then read the scripture, slowly but accurately.

President Stohlton thought little more of this until that afternoon, when the senior companion took an opportunity to bear his testimony. He started by saying, "Today you saw a miracle," and then he explained what he meant.

Through that testimony and other sources, President Stohlton learned the whole story. The missionary he had called on and the elder who had tried to stop him were actually brothers, named Chapman. They were from Perth, Australia, the sons of a stake president. Many years earlier, the young President Chapman had been considered a slow child, with little chance to succeed in life. He had married a local young woman who was a returned missionary. She had served in Australia in the 1960s under Elder Bruce R. McConkie. At the time of his marriage President Chapman was working for a railroad, but he decided he wanted to study law. His own father thought the pursuit worthless because of the young man's problems. However, the "slow" young man not only finished law school but rose to prominence in his field.

His second son, Adam, was also considered slow in school. He was eventually diagnosed as dyslexic. When he left school, he could hardly read at all. But when President Chapman set Adam apart as a missionary, he blessed him that he would be able to read and comprehend the Book of Mormon. When Adam arrived in the mission field, he was placed with his brother, Peter, so that someone who understood his difficulty could help him get by. He had been on his mission only a short time when President Stohlton called on him at the conference to read the scripture.

For a dyslexic, written symbols reverse themselves in the reader's mind and confusion sets in. Without knowing anything of this condition, President Stohlton had called upon the young missionary to read in front of a sizable group, and his older brother had tried to save him the embarrassment that was sure to follow. But young Adam Chapman trusted in his father's blessing, and he stood and read the words. What Peter knew was that Adam had never before been able to do such a thing—and that a miracle had occurred.

This was only the beginning. In the following months, Adam Chapman read the Book of Mormon from cover to cover. He understood everything he read. At the same time, his confidence took a great leap forward.

Adam Chapman served a fine mission. He had a wonderful, sweet spirit, and he was always willing to do whatever was asked of him. As he reached the end of his mission, he had a great desire to serve as a trainer for a new missionary. This meant a great deal to him, and President Stohlton was convinced that he could now do it. On the day Elder Chapman received notice that he would receive a new missionary, however, he called President Stohlton and told him that he would like, if possible, to stay with his current companion.

President Stohlton, knowing of Elder Chapman's desire to become a trainer, pressed him for a reason. Elder Chapman explained that his current companion was still suffering because of the death of his father. He felt that if the two stayed together he could help his companion through this hard time, and the younger missionary would be able to complete his mission.

Elder Adam Chapman had learned more on his mission than how to read the Book of Mormon. By sacrificing his own desires to meet the needs of someone else, he proved that he had come to comprehend the *meaning* of the Book of Mormon— just as his father had promised. He understood the gospel of Jesus Christ.

This chapter is based on interviews with John Stohlton by Dean Hughes, February 1995; and unpublished letters in possession of John Stohlton.

25

PIONEERING IN RUSSIA—WITH A BONUS

Early missionaries often had the chance to take the gospel to new lands, to preach where no LDS missionary had ever served before. For the last several decades, few missionaries have had that opportunity. But in recent years, entirely new areas of the world have opened up, and our missionaries have again been able to set foot in new places—to be modern pioneers.

Elder Jared Damiano, a young man from Oregon, was one of those modern missionaries who had the chance to open a new field of labor. He actually served in three different missions in two years. In 1991 he was called to the Finland Helsinki East Mission, which included Moscow, before the Church received permission to set up a headquarters in Russia. When a mission was opened in Russia, he was transferred there. And later, when that mission was divided, he became part of the Russia Saratov Mission.

When he served in Zelenograd, about thirty miles from Moscow, he was breaking new ground. He and three other missionaries were the first to serve in that city of 250,000 people.

Russian missionaries were not allowed to go door to door. Two men in dark suits knocking on a door called to mind too many bad experiences with KGB officers. However, the missionaries found success in setting up street displays, with pictures and scriptures to attract the attention of those walking by.

One day Elder Damiano and his companion were standing at their display when a young man named Arthur Kiejan stopped to talk to them. They were accustomed to many people stopping to try out their English. They had no reason to think that Arthur was any different. In fact, when Arthur asked, in perfect English, whether the missionaries could help him get an English-language Bible, they suspected his interest was more in the language than in the things they had to teach. But Arthur told them he had been investigating many religions and was looking for the truth. He had been searching for many years. The elders hoped he was sincere about that.

That night, the elders called the people they had met during the day. Elder Damiano left a message with Arthur's mother. He invited the young man to attend church the next morning. The elders were pleased when he called back a little later and said he would be there. But many make promises. The elders were even more pleased when they saw Arthur come in and take a seat in the back of the chapel.

Elder Damiano was serving as first counselor in the branch presidency, so he was sitting up front. When the meeting ended, though, Arthur didn't slip away. He waited to talk to the missionaries. Arthur told the missionaries that he listened carefully to everything he had heard in Sunday School and sacrament meeting. He told them again that he had been searching for the truth for a long time. Then he said he thought he had found it in what he had heard that day. Now he wanted to learn everything about the Church.

Needless to say, the missionaries were overjoyed. They taught him the missionary lessons over the next two weeks, and Arthur Kiejan was baptized. Four months after his baptism he was president of the Sunday School. He later married a member of the Church, and by 1995 he was attending BYU, where he was working on a graduate degree in business administration. When he returns to Russia, he will surely become a great asset to the Church in that country.

Elder Damiano and his companions had many other experiences of this kind. The Russian people had been starved for the free expression of religion during the years when communism dominated their lives. Many, like Arthur, were searching for something to give them a deeper understanding and satisfaction in life. In 1991, when Elder Damiano arrived in Moscow, there were only thirty-six members of the Church in the city. He was one of twenty-four missionaries. By the time he left Russia in 1993, there were ninety-nine missionaries in Moscow alone, and there were seven hundred members in eighteen branches. This great pioneering effort had brought forth wonderful fruits very quickly, and the gospel continues to spread across a country that was not allowed to experience the fullness of the gospel for many decades.

Elder Damiano was also involved in another important event that spread awareness of the Church throughout Russia—and, as it turned out, the experience came with a personal bonus. While he was serving in Saratov, the Young Ambassadors from Brigham Young University toured the nation and stopped in his city. The group was featured on television, and their performances brought much positive attention to the Church. Elder Dennis B. Neuenschwander of the Seventy accompanied their tour and had many opportunities to explain the basic doctrines of the Church.

After the performance in Saratov, the Young Ambassadors were boarding their bus and the missionaries were helping load the baggage. Elder Damiano heard someone singing. He turned to see where that beautiful voice was coming from. When he looked at Tiffany Crabtree, he had the distinct feeling that he had met her before. He asked her whether they had met, but neither could think where it might have been. They told each other their names, and that was that.

Except that it wasn't *entirely* that. For neither could forget the other.

When Tiffany got back to BYU, she spoke with a girl named Jenny, a good friend from Portland, Oregon. She said she had met an elder in Russia whose last name started with a *D*. He was from a town in Oregon that was close to Portland, and it started with a *T*. He was tall and blond—and, well, she wondered whether she would ever see him again.

Jenny didn't know the elder, but she didn't have long to wait before she came across him. One Sunday, when she was home in Portland, she picked up a program from the ward that had met previously in the same building where she attended church. On the program was an announcement of a fireside. Jared Damiano, from Tigard, would talk about his missionary experiences in Russia. As it turned out, Jenny's sister-in-law knew Elder Damiano's mother. She called and told the elder's mother that Tiffany Crabtree had never forgotten her son.

When Elder Damiano got the news, he was stunned. He had kept the Young Ambassadors program. He had not forgotten Tiffany—but he had assumed that she had forgotten him. Now he had her phone number at BYU.

Elder Damiano made some great friends during his mission. He and Arthur Kiejan will be friends forever. But he and Tiffany are even closer. They are now married. He had a wonderful experience in Russia—with a bonus.

This chapter is based on interviews with Jared Damiano by Tom Hughes, March 1995.

26

THE FAITH OF THE UGANDANS

In 1993, Larry and Ann Francis of Provo, Utah, like hundreds of other retired couples, began eighteen months of missionary service. They had not planned to leave quite so soon, but suddenly things fell together, and they felt that the Lord wanted them to serve at that very time. As they waited for their call, they visited the Church historical museum in Salt Lake City. While viewing a display on the Church in Africa, both found themselves responding powerfully, even shedding tears. They felt connected to the good brothers and sisters who were building the Church on that continent.

Two days later they received their call—to the Kenya Nairobi Mission.

The mission included not only Kenya but Uganda, Tanzania, and Ethiopia, all in eastern Africa. Since Larry was retiring from a career as a dentist, and Ann as a dental assistant, they were called to offer their health skills for half of each day and to proselyte during the remaining hours. They would live in Kampala, Uganda. At the very time that the Francises had seen things "fall together" so that they could accept a mission call, those running the health program in Uganda had been praying that a dentist would appear among missionary applicants. An LDS dentist in Uganda had died, and the program was in desperate need of help.

The Francises had to make some major adjustments when they arrived in Kampala. The house, part of a compound left from the British colonial era, was a block building with concrete floors. Food was readily available, but everything had to be cooked from scratch. Conditions were not terrible, but they certainly weren't like home, and children and grandchildren were far away. The Francises had some serious doubts for a time whether they had done the right thing.

Elder and Sister Francis soon realized, however, that they lived in splendor compared to most people. The most common home for Ugandans was a one-room structure, and the average person was lucky to earn the equivalent of thirty dollars a month. The poverty and hardship these people endured were heartbreaking, but Larry and Ann soon discovered nobility and great faith in the Ugandans they came to know.

The Francises had many great experiences, but perhaps the story of a young woman named Alex Sempa best explains why they came to love their mission. Alex lived alone with her two children. The father of the children had more or less abandoned her. She survived by cooking and selling *samosas*—a meat-filled pastry much like a Chinese wonton. Her earnings were meager, and she lived in a little two-room dwelling above a store in a rough area of Kampala. Drunks often sprawled on the rickety stairway, and her rooms, though neat and clean, were squalid by any standards. Mice ran about on the floors. A window was broken. Furniture was old and inadequate.

Larry and Ann met Alex when she showed up at the rented building where church was held. Alex had been a member of the Church of Uganda all her life, but one Sunday she arrived at services only to be told that she couldn't come in. Someone had paid money for her pew, and she no longer had a place to sit. She knew this could not be God's will, and she wondered where she might find a church that was truly of God.

One day Alex discussed her concerns with a friend who worked in a local hotel. The friend told Alex that she had seen a man of God. The man, as it turned out, was Larry K. Brown, the mission president. Whenever he came to Kampala, he stayed in the hotel. The woman had watched him, experienced his kindness and goodness, and sensed something godly about him. She told Alex where the man's church was.

The Francises had learned that they didn't have to go looking for people to teach. Ugandans came to the church constantly, asking questions. Between these visitors and referrals from members, the missionaries were kept busy. But when Alex showed up, they soon knew she was someone special. They sensed her intelligence and sincerity.

When Elder and Sister Francis first visited in Alex's home, they found that she had an eight-year-old daughter named Judith and a four-year-old son named Emmanuel. Emmanuel was suffering from a severe neurological disorder. He would thrash about constantly, banging his head and arms. Alex had taken him to the best doctors in Kampala, but no one had been able to help him. He was taking medication, but it seemed to have little effect.

Elder Francis asked Alex whether she believed that Jesus had healed the sick and the lame, and she said she did. He explained to her that he had the same power Jesus possessed, and that he would be willing to bless her son. Alex immediately expressed her faith that he could be healed, and so Elder Francis blessed the little boy.

Elder Larry Francis and Sister Ann Francis with Ugandan converts

A few days later, the Francises returned to find Emmanuel greatly improved. By the time they left Uganda, Emmanuel was a normal boy. He was taking no medications, and he was running and playing like any other child.

But this was only the first of the miracles. The Francises continued to teach Alex and her children. Alex Sempa and her daughter, Judith, were baptized, and within a short time Sister Sempa became the Primary president in the branch. She was reliable, and she was good to the children.

One day Elder and Sister Francis returned from their weekly "outreach" trip, on which they did dental work for orphans. They learned that Judith had fallen on a sharp object and had badly injured her eye. A doctor had concluded that the eye would have to be removed since it was so badly torn and penetrated. Elder Francis asked Sister Sempa to delay the surgery, and he sought out an eye specialist he had become acquainted with.

The next day, Sunday, Elder Francis and another priesthood holder anointed and blessed Judith. On Monday, the eye surgeon took the bandage off her eye, expecting to see a terrible injury. But the eye had healed. A small scar was all that was left of the injury. Within a few months, even the scar had disappeared.

The crisis was over, but a new one followed. Sister Sempa learned that because she had spent so much time at the hospital, she had lost her contract to cook *samosas*. She had no idea how she would continue to feed her children. When Elder and Sister Francis told her to pay her tithing on what she did have and to hold to the principles of the Church, she obeyed. Within a few days she received a contract that was much better than the one she had been working under. Her situation was actually improved.

Through this experience, Judith's faith became as sincere as her mother's. On one occasion, as she was going to buy ingredients for the *samosas* that her mother cooked, she lost her purse in a busy market area. This was an area full of thieves and vagrants. For three days Judith kept praying and looking. There seemed no way that the purse could still be in that marketplace. But on the third day she found it—with all the money still inside.

The Francises had many other remarkable experiences. Elder Francis administered to a woman who was very near death from malaria. They returned that afternoon to find her up and well. They baptized many people, and they saw miracles happen in those new members' lives as well.

They also experienced enormous satisfaction from the dental service they offered. In one case, they were able to restore the palate—the roof of the mouth—and repair the badly cleft lip of a boy named Ikoba, who had been treated as a freak in his village. When they returned Ikoba to his home, the village came out to look at the boy and to stare at him in wonder. Ikoba was overjoyed to be normal and accepted. His parents presented the Francises with a beautiful wooden stool—and a goat. The goat they could have lived without, but they knew it would be rude to turn it down, so they accepted it and took it back to Kampala.

When the Francises' mission came to an end, they were crying again. This time they were shedding tears because they had to leave all their dear friends in

Uganda. Elder and Sister Francis had accepted a mission call because they wanted to teach the gospel and offer blessings through their dental skills. They returned with deeper faith and a deeper understanding of the gospel. Certainly, the Ugandans had blessed them as much as they had blessed the Ugandans. But then, as we have seen in all the accounts in this book, that is usually the case.

This chapter is based on interviews with Larry and Ann Francis by Dean Hughes, March 1995.